Excel
Basic Skills

English and Mathematics

Year 7
Ages 12-13

Get the Results You Want!

PASCAL PRESS

Contents

Introduction

The *Excel* Basic Skills Workbook series aims to build and reinforce basic skills in reading, comprehension and mathematics.

The series has eight English and Mathematics core books, one for each of the school years Kindergarten/Foundation to Year 7. These are supported by teaching books, which can be used if the student needs help in a particular area of study.

The structure of this book

This book has 30 carefully sequenced double-page units. Each unit has work on Number, Algebra, Measurement, Space, Statistics and Probability in Maths, and Reading and Comprehension, Spelling and Vocabulary, and Grammar and Punctuation in English.

The student's competence in each of the 30 units can be recorded on the marking grid on pages 5 and 7. There are four end-of-term reviews. These are referred to as Tests 1 to 4. They assess the student's understanding of work covered during each term.

How to use this book

It is recommended that students complete each unit in the sequence provided because the knowledge and understanding developed in each unit is consolidated and practised in subsequent units. The workbook can be used to cover core classroom work. It can also be used to provide homework and consolidation activities.

All units are written so that particular questions deal with the same areas of learning in each unit. For example, question 1 is always on Number and question 12 is always on Measurement (time), and so on. Similarly in the English units question 1 is always on Reading and Comprehension, and question 14 is always on Punctuation. Question formatting is repeated throughout the workbook to support familiarity so that students can more readily deal with the Mathematics and English content.

The marking grids (see the examples on pages 4 and 6) are easy-to-use tools for recording students' progress. If you find that certain questions are repeatedly causing difficulties and errors, then there is a specific *Excel* Basic/Advanced/Essential Skills Workbook to help students fully revise that topic.

These are the teaching books of the series; they will take students through the topic step by step. The use of illustrations and diagrams, practice questions, and a straightforward and simple approach will make some of the most common problem areas of English and Mathematics easy to understand and master.

Sample Maths Marking Grid

If a student is consistently getting more than **one in five** questions wrong in any area, refer to the highlighted *Excel* **Basic/Advanced/Essential Skills** title. When marking answers on the grid, simply mark incorrect answers with 'X' in the appropriate box. This will result in a graphical representation of areas needing further work. An example has been done below for the first seven units. If a question has several parts, it should be counted as wrong if one or more mistakes are made.

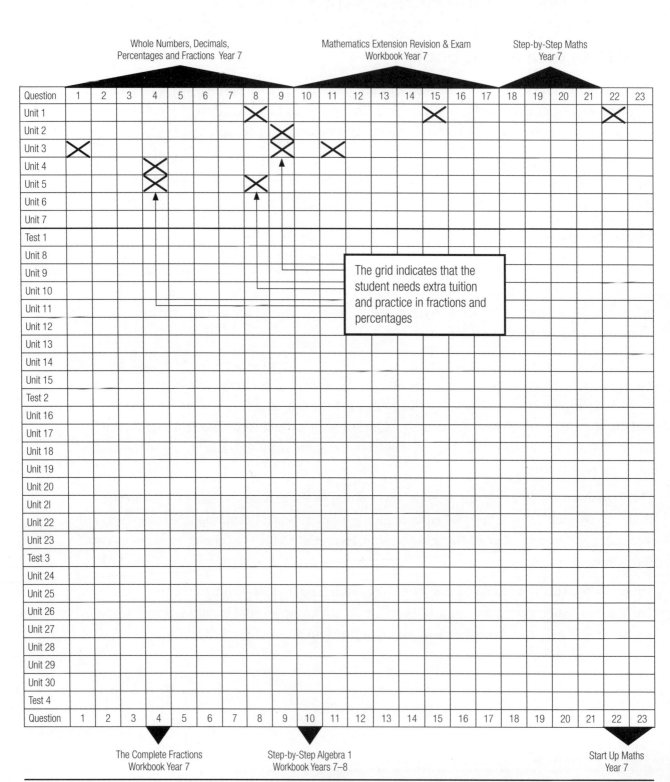

Whole Numbers, Decimals, Percentages and Fractions Year 7

Mathematics Extension Revision & Exam Workbook Year 7

Step-by-Step Maths Year 7

The grid indicates that the student needs extra tuition and practice in fractions and percentages

The Complete Fractions Workbook Year 7

Step-by-Step Algebra 1 Workbook Years 7–8

Start Up Maths Year 7

Maths Marking Grid

Question	Number Addition, Subtraction, Multiplication, Division			Fractions	Decimals	Operations—Whole Numbers	Operations—Decimals	Operations—Fractions	Percentages	Ratio	Algebra	Algebra	Algebra	Algebra	Time/Mass	Length	Area	Volume/Capacity	2D/3D Shapes	Angles	Probability	Statistics
	1	2	3	4	5	6	7	8	9	10	11	12	13	14	15	16	17	18	19	20	21	22
Unit 1																						
Unit 2																						
Unit 3																						
Unit 4																						
Unit 5																						
Unit 6																						
Unit 7																						
Test 1																						
Unit 8																						
Unit 9																						
Unit 10																						
Unit 11																						
Unit 12																						
Unit 13																						
Unit 14																						
Unit 15																						
Test 2																						
Unit 16																						
Unit 17																						
Unit 18																						
Unit 19																						
Unit 20																						
Unit 21																						
Unit 22																						
Unit 23																						
Test 3																						
Unit 24																						
Unit 25																						
Unit 26																						
Unit 27																						
Unit 28																						
Unit 29																						
Unit 30																						
Test 4																						
Question	1	2	3	4	5	6	7	8	9	10	11	12	13	14	15	16	17	18	19	20	21	22

Sample English Marking Grid

If a student is consistently getting more than one in five questions wrong in any area, refer to the highlighted *Excel* **Basic/Essential Skills** title. When marking answers on the grid, simply mark incorrect answers with 'X' in the appropriate box. This will result in a graphical representation of areas needing further work. An example has been done below for the first seven units.

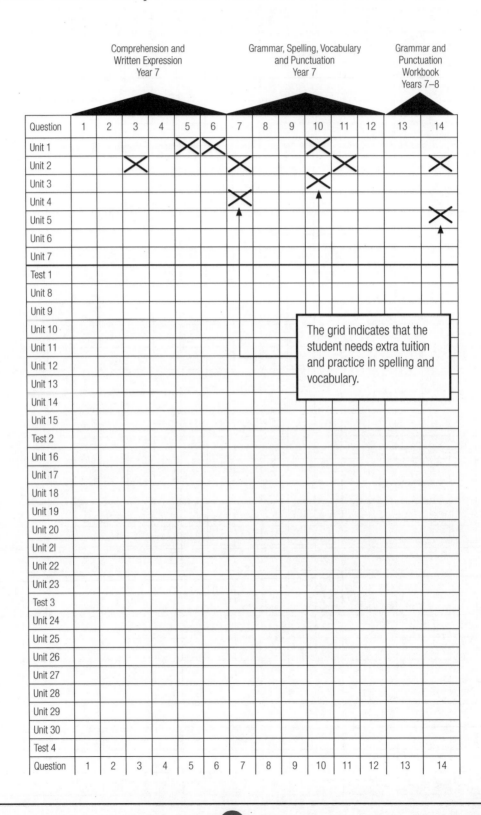

English Marking Grid

Question	Reading and Comprehension						Spelling and Vocabulary						Grammar and Punctuation	
	1	2	3	4	5	6	7	8	9	10	11	12	13	14
Unit 1														
Unit 2														
Unit 3														
Unit 4														
Unit 5														
Unit 6														
Unit 7														
Test 1														
Unit 8														
Unit 9														
Unit 10														
Unit 11														
Unit 12														
Unit 13														
Unit 14														
Unit 15														
Test 2														
Unit 16														
Unit 17														
Unit 18														
Unit 19														
Unit 20														
Unit 21														
Unit 22														
Unit 23														
Test 3														
Unit 24														
Unit 25														
Unit 26														
Unit 27														
Unit 28														
Unit 29														
Unit 30														
Test 4														
Question	1	2	3	4	5	6	7	8	9	10	11	12	13	14

Mathematics

Number and Algebra

1. Write 175.75 million in words.

   _____

2. Complete:

$x =$	5	6	7	8	9	10	11	12
$x + 4 =$								

3. List the ten digits.

   _____

   (a) Circle the composite digits.

   (b) Cross out those that are square.

4. Arrange these fractions in ascending order.
   $\frac{1}{4}, \frac{1}{5}, \frac{1}{2}, \frac{3}{10}, \frac{1}{20}$

   _____

5. Which is the largest number in this group?
   7.077, 7.7, 7.77, 7.007, 7.07 _____

6. What is the difference between three million and one hundred and forty thousand? _____

7. What is the sum of seven hundredths, 4.016 and 9.318? _____

8. (a) $3\frac{1}{3} + 2\frac{1}{6} =$ _____

   (b) $5\frac{3}{4} - 2\frac{3}{8} =$ _____

9. What sum of money is equal to 20% of $260? _____

10. Simplify $10 : 1000$. _____

11. The sum of two pronumerals (a and b) is $ab \,/\, a + b \,/\, \frac{a}{b} \,/\, b - a$. Circle the correct one.

12. What is the value of x in the following?

    (a) $64 \div x = x$ _____

    (b) $x^2 + 7 = 71$ _____

13. $4x \times 3y =$ _____

14. Complete the table for $y = 2x + 1$

x	0	1	2	3
y				

Measurement and Space

15. How many hours and minutes are there between 2:35 pm and midnight? _____

16. Each of the sides of this irregular shape has a length of 87 mm.

    What is the perimeter in metres?

    _____

17. A rectangular plot of land is 187 m by 52 m. How much more or less than a hectare is this area? _____

18. Find the missing dimension in this volume statement.

    $24\ cm^3 = 3\ cm \times$ _____ $cm \times 4\ cm$

19. Draw a net for a pyramid.

20. Write the measurements of each shaded angle in the triangle.

    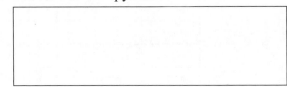

    _____

Statistics and Probability

21. Look at this spinner. How many possible outcomes are there?

    _____

    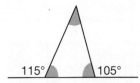

22. What is the mean of these scores? _____

    8   10   9   16   10   13

Who shot the wombat?

Who shot the wombat with the golden fur,
Which fed on open fields beside the sea . . .
Which shared the world with echidna,
possum, wallaby?
Who lifted a rifle to the shoulder,
Sighted, took aim?
Who toppled this marsupial trundler?
Who killed this grass-nibbling burrower?
Who forgot—and shot?
I killed the wombat. So what?
I shot the wombat. Why not?
I like wildlife too, you know,
I love our marsupials as much as the next man.
I only kill a few.
I try not to hit the females
But...
Wombats destroy the pasture for my sheep.
Wombats knock down fences, dig holes,
Holes which are dangerous for cattle and
sheep—
Break their legs.
I can't have that.
I only kill a few.
I try not to hit the females.
You understand don't you?
Don't you?

From *Golden Wombats* by Jill Morris

Reading and Comprehension

1. The marsupial mentioned in this poem is
(a) the trundler.   (b) the burrower.
(c) the sheep.   (d) the wombat.

2. It is certain that the hunter
(a) doesn't like wildlife.
(b) is afraid of females.
(c) only kills some wombats.
(d) is not a farmer but a killer.

3. What is a marsupial?

_____

4. Give two reasons why wombats would represent
a nuisance.
(a) _____
(b) _____

5. Why did the writer stress that he tried not to
shoot females?

_____

_____

6. Does the man get satisfaction from
shooting wildlife? Explain your answer.

_____

_____

Spelling and Vocabulary

Rewrite the misspelt words.

7. Brake there legs. _____

8. You understand dond you? _____

Circle the word that has the nearest meaning to the
underlined word.

9. Wombats destroy the <u>pasture</u> for my sheep.
(a) grazing ground   (b) path
(c) milk buckets   (d) passion

10. This animal is a grass-nibbling <u>burrower</u>.
(a) loaner   (b) beggar   (c) breaker   (d) digger

Circle the correct word in brackets.

11. The wombat has golden (fir / fur).

12. I (carnt / can't / cant) have that!

Grammar and Punctuation

13. Join these sentences by using *who*, *whose* or
which.
Here is the wombat. It destroyed my
fences.

_____

_____

14. Punctuate and capitalise this text.
i shot the wombat why not

_____

_____

Number and Algebra

1. What is the number seven times greater than the answer to this operation?

   $(4 \times 7) + 2 - (18 - 7)$ _____

2. Write one number for 400 + 9 units + 37 hundredths and seven thousandths.

   _____

3. (a) List the first five multiples of 8.

   _____

   (b) Now list the first five multiples of 12.

   _____

   (c) Which multiples are common?

   _____

   (d) Of those, which is the Lowest Common Multiple (LCM)? _____

4. Change 3.15 to fraction form. _____

5. Show where 3.2 and 5.7 fall on this number line. Label them *A* and *B*.

   ```
   0   1   2   3   4   5   6
   +---+---+---+---+---+---+
   ```

6. Subtract 3.872 from 10.1. _____

7. Divide 16.485 by 7. _____

8. What is the sum of $3\frac{1}{5}$ and $2\frac{1}{2}$? _____

9. What sum of money is 15% of $86? _____

10. Simplify the ratio 4:24 _____

11. I have 4 boxes of books, each holding *x* books. If I take out 3 books, how many have I now? Choose the correct algebraic expression to represent this.

    $x - 4 + 3$, $4x + 3$, $4x - 3$ _____

12. If *l* = 6 and *m* = 9, then $2l + 3m =$ _____

13. Simplify $3a + 4b - a - b$. _____

14. Mark the position at (3, 4) as X.

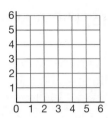

Measurement and Space

15. Use am or pm to write 9 past 11 in the morning. _____

16. How many 30-cm lengths of lace can be cut from a 5-m roll? Discard the leftover lace. _____

17. 2.3 m² is the same area as _____ cm² or _____ mm².

18. Here is a cubic block of concrete. One edge measures 182 cm. Use your calculator to find the volume of this shape in m³.

    _____

19. Is the surface *DCGF* perpendicular or parallel to the surface *CBAD*?

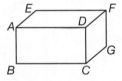

    _____

20. $\angle a$ and $\angle b$ are complementary angles. If $\angle a$ is 37° less than a right angle, $\angle b$ must be equal to _____.

Statistics and Probability

21. A bag contains 6 balls. Four of the balls are red and there is an equal number of blue and green balls. A ball is chosen at random. What is the probability that it is blue?

    _____

22. Here are 5 scores.

    17, 10, 18, 22, 9

    What is the median of the scores?

    _____

Ho, Ho, Ho!

Poor old Santa sighed sadly and said,
… 'I guess I'd have to be pretty dim
To think that wishing would make me slim.
So if I'm to be on that special flight,
I'll have to agree to do what is right.
I promise that every single day
I'll follow the program in every way.'
The elves looked away whenever he moaned,
And covered their ears each time he groaned.
They watched Santa run, jog, skip, ride and row,
And fight with the fridge, his deadliest foe.
In a week which seemed like a year and a day,
They watched Santa's kilograms fade away.
Mrs Claus had finally proved she was right:
The excess fat had vanished from sight!
Now slim Santa shouted, 'You little beaut!
At last I fit into my working suit.
No longer am I as round as a ball—
In fact, I now have no problem at all!
But listen to me, all you girls and boys:
When I come around to deliver your toys,
Forget about leaving out cake and beer—
I don't need that kind of Christmas cheer!'

From Ho, Ho, Ho! by Jan Weeks

Reading and Comprehension

1. In the phrase *his deadliest foe*, *foe* means
   (a) fridge.   (b) fat.
   (c) enemy.   (d) exercise regime.

2. Which activity was not a method used by Santa to lose weight?
   (a) running
   (b) swimming
   (c) avoiding the refrigerator
   (d) rowing

3. To which special flight does Santa refer?
   _____

4. How long did it take Santa to show noticeable weight loss?
   _____

5. In which order did these events occur?
   [1] [2] [3] [4] establishing an exercise routine
   [1] [2] [3] [4] feeling fabulous
   [1] [2] [3] [4] accepting the problem
   [1] [2] [3] [4] losing fat

6. Which of these statements is implied but not stated?
   (a) Santa is a long-distance runner.
   (b) The elves had a hearing problem.
   (c) Santa was not fit enough to deliver the presents.
   (d) It took Santa a year and one day to lose weight.

Spelling and Vocabulary

Rewrite the misspelt words.

7. Access kilograms disapeared from sight.

   _____

8. Santa had no problem fitting into his soot.

   _____

Circle the word that has the nearest meaning to the underlined word.

9. The elves gave three <u>cheers</u>.
   (a) drinks   (b) shouts   (c) claps   (d) blows

10. Mrs Claus established Santa's <u>program</u>.
    (a) flight   (b) plan   (c) fitness   (d) meals

Circle the correct word in brackets.

11. She was given a (choral / coral) necklace.

12. The Christmas (freeze / frieze) in the hall is very attractive.

Grammar and Punctuation

13. Give the singular form of the following words.
    fungi _____ termini _____

14. Punctuate and capitalise this sentence.

    santa had to run jog skip row and diet till christmas day

    _____

    _____

Number and Algebra

1. Write the number made up of 37 tenths, 58 tens and 14 thousandths. _____

2. Add the correct sign (>, < or =) to make this statement true.

   -14 _____ -37

3. Here is a number: forty-seven and eighty-nine thousandths. Round the number to the nearest hundredth and write as a decimal. _____

4. Here is a set of common fractions. Rearrange the order so that they are from least to greatest.

   $\frac{17}{24}, \frac{5}{6}, \frac{3}{8}, \frac{1}{4}, \frac{1}{3}$ _____

5. On a number line, what number lies midway between -7 and $+3$? _____

6. Add 37 416 to the product of 105 and 27. _____

7. Multiply 4.28 by 9 and then subtract the result from 50. _____

8. How much less than $100 is $11.65? _____

9. A farmer sold 20% of his flock of 2635 sheep. How many has he left? _____

10. A bag has 10 balls. Seven of the balls are red and the rest blue. What is the ratio of red balls to blue balls? _____

11. Prove that $3a(a + 5) = 3a^2 + 15a$ by substituting 3 for the unknown.

    _____

12. Find the value of y.
    $5y + 9 = 34$ _____

13. In a paddock there are x ducks and y sheep. What is the total number of legs? _____

14. Add $4p - q$ to $p + 3q$. _____

Measurement and Space

15. Write thirty-five minutes past seven in the evening in:

    • digital time _____

    • twenty-four hour time _____

16. The perimeter of a rectangle with side 25 cm is 96 cm.

    25 cm

    What is the width? _____

17. What is the area of a square with a side of 9.2 m? Use your calculator. _____

18. A prism is 4 cm long, 4 cm wide and 2 cm high. What is its volume? _____

19. How many centres has any circle? _____

20. There is one internal reflex angle inside this shape. Mark it on the drawing and name it.

    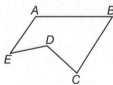

    _____

Statistics and Probability

21. A cube that has one of the letters A, B, C, D, E and F on each face is thrown. What is the probability of the F landing face down?

    _____

22. The mean of six scores is 9. What is the sum of the scores? _____

Brahmagupta and the frog

A legend from northern India, the year 640 CE:
Brahmagupta was the head astronomer. He sat with his students in the shade of a banyan tree. He was giving a lesson on positive and negative numbers. This was an important field of mathematics, which he had just discovered. He explained, 'If I make a profit, then I'm richer than before. That's positive. If I'm in debt, then I'm poor. That's negative. If I increase my profits, that's positive positive. If I decrease my profits that's negative positive ...'

The students squirmed. They were bored.

'A merchant bought some goats for 175 rupees on credit. That means he had a debt of 175 rupees. After selling some goats, the merchant was able to decrease this debt by 160 rupees. How much did the merchant still owe?' Brahmagupta asked.

No-one replied.

'A debt of 175 rupees is –175 and a decrease of the debt by 160 rupees is – –160, or a repayment of 160 rupees: + 160. So we have –175 – –160, which is –175 + 160 = –15 rupees, still a debt of 15 rupees!'

From *Additional Fables* by Rolf Grunseit

Reading and Comprehension

1. The year mentioned in the text was
   (a) 640 years after the Birth of Christ.
   (b) six hundred and four years ago.
   (c) another duration in time.
   (d) around summertime.

2. India's currency is known as the
   (a) banyan.   (b) rupee.
   (c) debt.   (d) rupees.

3. Who was Brahmagupta?

   _____

4. What does *buying the goats on credit* mean?

   _____

5. For what price did the merchant sell the goats?

   _____

6. Why do you think the astronomer is using the example of a debt incurred by a merchant in explaining positives and negatives to students?

   _____

   _____

Spelling and Vocabulary

Rewrite the misspelt words.

7. Too negatives don't make a right.

   _____

8. The sent of jasmine filled the observatory.

   _____

Circle the word that has the nearest meaning to the underlined word.

9. I need <u>positive</u> proof that Tom did it.
   (a) good   (b) poor
   (c) profit   (d) definite

10. There's no <u>profit</u> in being a thief.
    (a) motive   (b) loss
    (c) advantage   (d) proof

Circle the correct word in brackets.

11. The roses were (sent / scent) by my Valentine.

12. Sally was given good (advise / advice) by the Principal.

Grammar and Punctuation

13. Make these into compound sentences by adding another clause.
    (a) Louise strolled through the park and

    _____ .

    (b) Gordon will run here to

    _____ .

14. Punctuate and capitalise this text.

    thats positive thats negative

    _____

Number and Algebra

1. Use partitioning to divide 12 484 by 4.

$12\,000 \div 4 =$ _____ $400 \div 4 =$ _____

$80 \div 4 =$ _____ $4 \div 4 =$ _____

so $12\,484 \div 4 =$ _____ + _____

+ _____ + _____ = _____

2. Write 2 483 006 in words.

_____

3. If $\frac{3}{4}$ of 240 is 180, what is 0.25 of 180? _____

4. Which answer is greater? Circle it.

$(3 \times 5) \times 8 + 7^2 - 9 \div 3$

$(4 \times 6) + 7 + 6^2 + \frac{1}{3}$ of 15

5. What number lies 5 divisions to the right of zero? _____

```
 ┬───┬───┬───┬───┬───┬───┬───┬───┬───┬───┬───┬───┬
 -6  -5  -4  -3  -2  -1   0  +1  +2  +3  +4  +5  +6
```

6. Add 138 217 to 59 793 and subtract the result from 0.5 million. _____

7. What is the product of 7.135 and the difference between $\frac{3}{7}$ of 14 and $\frac{5}{8}$ of 24? _____

8. (a) $3\frac{1}{2} - 2\frac{1}{3} =$ (b) $6\frac{5}{8} + 2\frac{3}{4} =$

_____ _____

9. What is 15% of 14 800 tonnes expressed in kilograms? _____

10. What is the missing number?

_____ : 18 = 5 : 6

11. $(a + b) + c = a + (b + c)$. Use these values $(a = 5, b = 7, c = 9)$ to prove that this equation is either true or false. ☐ True ☐ False

12. This square has a side of b centimetres.

The area in m² is

$\frac{b}{100}, \frac{b^2}{100}$ or $\frac{b^2}{10\,000}$.

b cm

Circle the correct answer.

13. Solve the equation $3m + 4 = 19$. _____

14. How far did the cyclist travel in n hours?

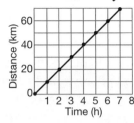

_____

Measurement and Space

15. If a driver weighs 97 kg, a prime mover and trailer 13 589 kg and the load 20 474 kg, what is the gross vehicle mass (truck, trailer, load and driver) in tonnes? _____

16. Find the perimeter of a triangle with sides $4x$ cm, $3x$ cm and $5y$ cm. _____

17. AB is 18 cm, BC is 12 cm. The area of the rectangle $ABCD$ is _____ .

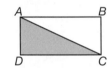

Use this fact to work out the area of the shaded triangular section DAC. _____

18. What is the difference in volume between twenty two-litre drums and a twenty-two-litre drum? _____

19. How many faces does this hexagonal prism have?

_____

20. There are 3 adjacent angles $\angle a$, $\angle b$ and $\angle c$. $\angle a = 52°$. $\angle a$ and $\angle b$ are complementary. $\angle a$, $\angle b$ and $\angle c$ are supplementary. Therefore $\angle b =$ _____ and $\angle c =$ _____ .

Statistics and Probability

21. What is the probability of selecting a vowel from this envelope? _____

22. What is the range of the scores shown in the dot plot?

_____

```
                  •
      •     •     •     •
      •     •     •     •
     ─┼─────┼─────┼─────┼─
      10    11    12    13
```

Good decision

It was one of those stinking hot days when all you wanted was to go to the beach. But after a couple of months of winter, one glance in the mirror told me I didn't really have the appropriate physique for stripping off on the sand. Because it was so sultry I thought why not—I'm going anyway.

Arriving at the beach I noticed a new building attached to the Surf Club. A new gymnasium had been built. Called 'Body Focus', it had several large plate glass windows facing the beach. Keen to check it out I went over to the main window. Inside were several body-builders working out on their biceps, triceps and who-knows-what-other-ceps.

All the equipment looked really great. There were some neat high-tech, multi-purpose machines, I thought maybe I'd like to try. There was even a free offer of one month's trial. Sounded interesting!

Once again I glanced at the many different kinds of machine. If they can do it, so can I! I watched one guy who was doing bench presses with three plates on each side of the bar. If they're 20 kilo plates, that's over 120 kilos—twice my weight!

Yes, I would enrol, I decided, but first a cool surf was needed. After that I'd see the fitness instructor for my first work-out. The decision had been made.

Reading and Comprehension

1. The writer was
   (a) feeling the heat.
   (b) travelling by car.
   (c) interested in the new building.
   (d) both (a) and (c)

2. The number of plates on either end of the bench press bar was
   (a) three.
   (b) twenty.
   (c) one hundred and twenty.
   (d) sixty.

3. What was the name of the gymnasium?

   _____

4. What free offer was available to new members?

   _____
   _____

5. Does the writer somehow believe he is inadequate? If so, explain.

   _____

6. Arrange in correct chronological order.
   (a) looking over the gymnasium   _____
   (b) having a refreshing surf   _____
   (c) making the decision to enrol   _____
   (d) arriving at the beach   _____

Spelling and Vocabulary

Rewrite the misspelt words.

7. Our Dutch nieghbours are boxing chanpions.

   _____

8. I was thankfull that the ordeel was over.

   _____

Circle the word that has the nearest meaning to the underlined word.

9. My cousins romped in the sand.
   (a) frolicked   (b) roamed
   (c) rested   (d) settled

10. Ill health compelled him to take up exercise.
    (a) prevented   (b) obliged   (c) thwarted   (d) forced

Circle the correct word in brackets.

11. The gymnasium made a good (prophet / profit) last year.

12. Many new roads were built on that vast (tracked / tract) of land.

Grammar and Punctuation

13. Change these two words to abstract nouns.
    (a) happy   _____
    (b) free   _____

14. Punctuate and capitalise this text.

    well said our aerobics teacher whos ready for some cardiovascular training

    _____
    _____

Number and Algebra

1. Complete:

$x =$	3	5	6	7	9
$x^2 - 3 =$					

2. Write one number for five billion, 36 ten thousands and 140 tens.

   _____

3. Arrange in descending order.
   38.011, 38.01, 38.001, 38.101, 38.111

   _____

4. Write a fraction equivalent to $\frac{24}{100}$. _____

5. Which directed number is halfway between −7 and 23? _____

6. $4 \times 5 \times 8 \times 3 = 20 \times A$ A = _____

   $ = 40 \times B$ B = _____

   $ = 32 \times C$ C = _____

7. From 19 ones subtract the sum of 4.138 and 5.729. _____

8. What is the sum of $5\frac{1}{8}$ and $3\frac{7}{16}$? _____

9. What is the difference in value?
   42% of $10 000 and 51% of $5000 _____

10. The ratio of balls to boxes is 4 : 3. If there are 12 balls, how many boxes are there? _____

11. I simplified the algebraic expression $\frac{25y}{100}$ to $\frac{5y}{2}$. Prove by substitution of 7 for y that this simplification is true or false.
    ☐ True   ☐ False

12. What is half of $6x$? _____

13. The line is translated 5 units to the right.

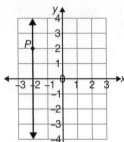

What is the new location of point P?

_____

14. Find the value of y.
    $\frac{3}{4}y + 17 = 26$ _____

Measurement and Space

15. The net mass of a bottle of mayonnaise is 150 g. The mass of the bottle is 35 g. What is the gross mass? _____

16. A rectangle has a length 10 times greater than its width. If the width is 89 mm, what is the perimeter in cm? _____

17. A circle has a diameter of 12.5 cm. What is the length of the radius? _____

18. The general formula to find the volume of a solid is Area of Base × Height. A shape has a rectangular base 7 cm long, 52 mm wide and a height of 8.1 cm. What is the volume?
    _____ cm³

19. What are the main differences between a square prism and a square pyramid?

    _____

    _____

20. In a diagram there are two adjacent angles $\angle ABC$ and $\angle DBC$. Together their sum is 120°. The difference between the two is 20°. If $\angle ABC$ is the larger angle, what is the size of $\angle DBC$? _____ degrees

Statistics and Probability

21. Look at the simple pointers made below. How many possible outcomes are there? For example, B4 is one outcome.

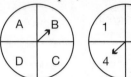

_____

22. Find the mean of these numbers:
    25, 100, 90, 75, 110, 90, 95, 80, 90, 55, 90, 60. _____

Interview

Int: Welcome again to 'Oz Talk'. Our guest for today is our State Business Manager of the Year, Mel Casperson. Welcome Mel!

Mel: Thanks Jerry—a pleasure to be here.

Int: Can you tell us about this award you've won?

Mel: Sure. It's given to the manager of a company for success in the marketplace and for helping the community.

Int: Your company, 'Elvin Industries', specialises in the manufacture of car seat covers. Is that correct?

Mel: Certainly is, Jerry. We began in 2005 and last year hit record export sales, almost $30 million.

Int: Congratulations. What percentage increase in turnover did you make?

Mel: Almost 60 per cent, so we are particularly pleased.

Int: Tell us about your community achievements.

Mel: Well, first we provided vehicles for the 'Meals on Wheels' scheme and bought a community bus for use by the retirees in Carnville. We think of them as very worthy of assistance. We also provided a children's playground at Carnville Kindergarten.

Int: No wonder you received the award. Congratulations and best wishes for next year.

Mel: Thanks Jerry.

Reading and Comprehension

1. The person interviewed was a
  (a) retiree.   (b) community representative.
  (c) business manager.   (d) bus driver.

2. During the year there was a 60% increase in
  (a) community work.   (b) vehicle donations.
  (c) turnover.   (d) kindergarten equipment.

3. What was the name of the company?

_____

4. What did the company provide for the Carnville Kindergarten?

_____

5. Explain in your own words why the award mentioned in the interview is of benefit to the country?

_____

_____

6. Arrange these phrases in the order in which the interviewer used them in his questioning.
  (a) increase in company turnover   _____
  (b) community achievements   _____
  (c) name and type of business   _____
  (d) reasons for award   _____

Spelling and Vocabulary

Rewrite the misspelt words.

7. I'd like a carere in poltics when I get older.

_____

8. The interviewer caried out some through reserch on the celebrity.

_____

Circle the word that has the nearest meaning to the underlined word.

9. Francesca told a downright lie.
  (a) devious   (b) unclear
  (c) indirect   (d) complete

10. Your commitment to this political party is sporadic.
  (a) continuous   (b) constant
  (c) irregular   (d) spotless

Circle the correct word in brackets.

11. William (purposely / purposefully) avoided seeing the Principal.

12. Try and find (further / farther) information on this topic.

Grammar and Punctuation

13. Is this sentence written in active or passive voice?
Rita has sent a card to her penpal.

_____

14. Punctuate and capitalise this sentence.
to my utter dismay councillor jones won the seat of griffith again

_____

_____

Number and Algebra

1. (a) Write the prime factors of 64.

_____

(b) $64 = $ _____ ^{2}

2. Arrange these in ascending order.
$-7, 2\frac{1}{4}, 5.75, -2.3, 47\%, -5.2$

_____

3. Use your calculator to convert $\frac{12}{15}$ to a decimal. _____

4. (a) Round 3.164 to the nearest hundredth. _____
(b) Round 15.787 to the nearest tenth. _____

5. Write the number for these in decimal form.
(a) $11 + \frac{4}{10} + \frac{7}{100} + \frac{3}{1000}$ _____
(b) $60 + 12 + \frac{11}{100} + \frac{5}{1000}$ _____

6. $[(6 \times 10 \times 26) + 7 \times 26] \div 26 = $ _____

7. _____ $- 0.68 = 4.3$

8. Add $3\frac{1}{4}$ and $\frac{15}{16}$. _____

9. Express each of the following percentages as a decimal fraction.
23% _____ 17% _____ 4% _____

10. In a pet shop the ratio of fish to birds is 11:3. If there are 66 fish, how many birds are there? _____

11. If $3(b-4)$ is the same as $3 \times b - 3 \times 4$, then what is $5(a+b)$? _____

12. What is the value of n if $30 - n = n$? _____

13. Simplify $12a \div 12$. _____

14. On the grid, mark in these coordinates.
A(1, 2), B(3, −2), C(2, −3), D(−1, −3)

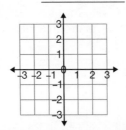

Measurement and Space

15. A mass of 0.065 tonnes is
_____ kg _____ grams.

16. How many cm are in 4.2 m? _____

17. Length 1 cm = _____ mm
Area 1 cm × 1 cm = _____ mm × _____ mm = _____ mm^2
Volume 1 cm × 1 cm × 1 cm = _____ mm × _____ mm × _____ mm = _____ mm^3

18. What is the difference in volume between these two shapes?

_____

19. True or false?
Every rectangle is a parallelogram. _____

20. In this shape there is an acute angle. Use the points given to name the angle in two ways.

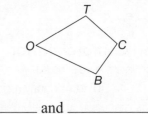

_____ and _____

Statistics and Probability

21. Using alphabet cards to explore probability, what chance is there of drawing the letter M?

_____

22. Students were asked to state the number of children in their families.
Replies are listed below:
3, 3, 5, 2, 4, 4, 3, 5, 2, 3, 3, 2, 4, 6, 2, 2, 3, 3, 4, 3, 5, 4, 3, 3, 3, 3.
What is the mode? _____

Bill the Bushy

Bill the Bushy lived in an old bark hut along the track that led to the goldfields. A happy, good-hearted sort of a bloke, he would always open his door to a traveller and would never see a mate go hungry. Not only was he a great host, he could spin a yarn like no-one else.

Like the time I stopped off to spend the night at Bill's on my way north for the shearing season. It was springtime, and unusually hot. Flies were swarming around me in droves as I walked along, and by the time I reached Bill's hut I was eager to get inside, away from their constant torment.

Bill opened the door and greeted me with his usual welcoming smile. 'G'day, mate! The billy's just boiled. As soon as you get rid of your travelling companions, I'll make you a cuppa.' He picked up a green twig, whisked away the mass of flies that covered my back, and bustled me through the door.

'Bad year for flies, by the looks of things', I said. Bill nodded. 'Get heavy, don't they? I remember one year', he said, with a twinkle in his eye, 'the flies were so bad that once a mob of them settled on your back, you had to stop and rest every once in a while because the sheer weight of them would make your knees buckle.'

From *Charlie's Fish* by RL Muddyman

Reading and Comprehension

1. Which of these statements about the Bushy is invalid?
    (a) He liked drinking tea.
    (b) He could tell a good story.
    (c) He lived in a shack.
    (d) His knees bent because of the flies' mass.

2. The *travelling companions* Bill refers to are
    (a) the tallest tales.
    (b) the other shearers.
    (c) the other nearby bushies.
    (d) the unwelcome droves of flies.

3. Which phrase means Bill told good stories?
    _____

4. What is the word *g'day* an abbreviation of?
    _____

5. Describe Bill the Bushy's character.
    _____
    _____

6. Which segment of the story shows gross exaggeration?
    _____

Spelling and Vocabulary

Rewrite the misspelt words.

7. Billy had such a wellcomeing smile.
    _____

8. I couldn't believe the shear wait of the books.
    _____

Circle the word that has the nearest meaning to the underlined word.

9. Bill the Bushy tantalised us with tales about buried treasure.
    (a) appeased   (b) satisfied
    (c) teased   (d) fulfilled

10. The mob walked away from the ferris wheel.
    (a) section   (b) group   (c) population   (d) crowd

Circle the correct word in brackets.

11. He bustled me (threw / through) the door.

12. Flies (where / was / were) swarming around the damper.

Grammar and Punctuation

13. Write a sentence using the past tense of *shearing*.
    _____
    _____

14. Punctuate and capitalise this sentence.

    billy said the mozzies settle down in a swamp to snooze through the days heat
    _____
    _____

Number and Algebra

1. (a) Write 307 904 in expanded notation.
    _____

    (b) Write 524 008 in exponential notation.
    _____

2. Supply the missing numbers.

    $11.725 =$ ____ $+ 1 + \dfrac{7}{\boxed{}} + \dfrac{\boxed{}}{100} +$ ____

3. Circle the numbers evenly divisible by 7.
    3969   2023   6923   11 307

4. (a) Round 26.107 to the
        nearest tenth.   _____
    (b) Round 5.387 to the
        nearest hundredth.   _____

5. Write in order from largest to smallest:
    +3, +6, −8, −2   _____

6. A series of 6 volumes of nature books
    has a total of 2070 pages. How many
    pages are there in two dozen sets
    of these books?   _____

7. What is the difference between 1024
    hundredths and 1042 thousandths? _____

8. What is the sum of $4\frac{1}{2}$ and $\frac{11}{12}$? _____

9. Use your calculator to find $12\frac{1}{2}\%$
    of $9886.48.   _____

10. There are 12 cats and 10 dogs. What is the
    simplified ratio of dogs to cats? _____

11. If x has a value of 2, what then is the value
    of this algebraic expression?
    $3(3x + x^2) + x =$ _____

12. $21 - n - n - n = 0$; $n =$ _____

13. Expand $2(a - 5)$.   _____

14. On the number plane,
    plot (2, 2), (2, −3)
    and (−2, −3).

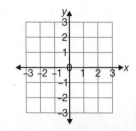

Measurement and Space

15. Write the time which is 15 minutes
    after 11:51 am.   _____

16. If the longest distance across a circular shape
    is 9.9 m, what is the radius of the shape?
                             _____

17. The front fence of a rectangular property is
    1728 m long. The depth of the property is
    2.82 km. Calculate the area of the property
    in both m² and ha.
    _____ and _____

18. A business sold fifty 200-millilitre containers
    of yoghurt and nineteen 250-millilitre
    containers of cream. How many litres were
    sold altogether?   _____

19. Name this shape. It has 5 sides, 8 equal
    edges, 5 corners and only one side is not a
    triangle.   _____

20. A line segment intersects two parallel line
    segments to form 8 angles.

    (a) Which angle is alternate to d? _____
    (b) h and g are _____ angles.

Statistics and Probability

21. From the basket of numbers, what is the
    probability of drawing an odd number?

                             _____

22. The results of a test were 16, 13, 18, 16, 15,
    19, 17.
    What was the mode
    of the results?   _____

Good Neighbour movement

The Good Neighbour movement was founded in 1949 to encourage Australians to help migrants to assimilate into the community. Good Neighbour Councils were set up in each of the states and annual Australian Citizenship Conventions were held to exchange ideas and information at a national level.

Local Good Neighbour groups were formed to help migrants moving in to their locality. Their work included organising social events where migrants could meet Australians, visiting migrants in hospital and encouraging Australians to open their homes to migrant visitors. They also introduced migrants to local facilities such as schools, churches and hospitals. 'By this practical approach to the problem of assimilation, Australia hopes to achieve the ideal of one national family', wrote Tasman Heyes, Secretary of the Immigration Department, in 1951.

Most of the people who worked for the Good Neighbour movement did so as unpaid volunteers. One of their main objectives was to encourage non–English speaking migrants to speak English.

From *Homeland Australia* by Michael Dugan

Reading and Comprehension

1. Why is this historical piece so important?
   (a) It helps historians make a clear image of the past.
   (b) It explains a strategy used to help achieve a united Australia.
   (c) It locates non–English speaking groups.
   (d) It explains how Australia's migration grew.

2. To change one's home to another region or country is to
   (a) assimilate.   (b) migrate.
   (c) immigrate.   (d) emigrate.

3. In the early fifties, what position did Heyes hold?

   _____

4. Which word in the text means 'a large assembly'?

   _____

5. In your opinion, what is meant by the *ideal of one national family*?

   _____

   _____

6. Why would one of the main objectives of the Good Neighbour movement be to encourage non–English speaking migrants to speak English?

   _____

   _____

Spelling and Vocabulary

Rewrite the misspelt words.

7. Australia is a multiculturel nation south of the equater.

   _____

8. Migrents ajusted well to the Australian way of life.

   _____

Circle the word that has the nearest meaning to the underlined word.

9. It will take some time to assimilate the data.
   (a) admire   (b) absorb   (c) attain   (d) arrange

10. Our Ethnic Festival is approaching fast.
    (a) commencing   (b) appointing
    (c) nearing   (d) appealing

Circle the correct word in brackets.

11. Ng and (I / me / myself) were encouraged to speak English.

12. They (allowed / aloud) the passengers to walk along the narrow (isle / aisle) beside the ship.

Grammar and Punctuation

13. Circle the nouns in this statement.

    There was a shortage of interpreters at all levels of the movement.

14. Punctuate and capitalise this sentence.

    government services had to cater for non English speaking migrants

    _____

    _____

Mathematics

Number and Algebra

1. Start with the first number then add 15 each time.

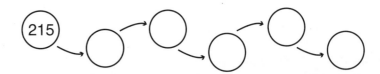

2. Complete:

$a =$	5	6	7	9	14	23	37	45
$a \times 3 =$								

3. Work your way back along this number line, subtracting 1.5 each time.

4. Arrange this set of common fractions in order from greatest to least.
$$\frac{16}{30}, \frac{5}{6}, \frac{1}{2}, \frac{11}{15}, \frac{2}{5}$$

_____

5. Take a further 87 from the answer after 26 has been subtracted from 55. Show the moves on this number line.

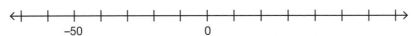

6. A mineshaft lift descended to level B (837 m below ground), then a further 189 m to level C and finally 302 m down to the lowest level in the mine. How much deeper than 1 km is this mine? _____ m

7. Lara's savings were increased from $17.50 by $39.20. Adele's were increased from $32.70 by $58.40. What is the total of the two girls' savings now? _____

8. Add $3\frac{1}{7}$ and $1\frac{1}{3}$. _____

9. What is 7% of 2.2 kilograms expressed in grams? _____

10. Circle the spinner that has been divided in the ratio $6:2:4$.

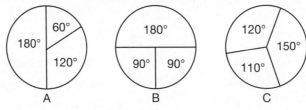

11. x boxes each contained y books. If all of those books were made into z stacks, how many were in each stack? Rewrite this as an algebraic expression.

_____

12. In a van there are 20 cartons with x articles in each and 9 cartons with y articles in each. Show in algebraic form the total number of cartons in the van. _____

13. Aaron solved the equation $x^2 = 25$. What are the two values of x? _____

14. Triangle *ABC* is translated 3 units to the right.

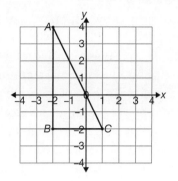

What are the coordinates of the
image of each vertex?

(__ , __), (__ , __), (__ , __)

Measurement and Space

15. A mass of 0.072 tonnes is _____ kg _____ grams.

16. The area of a square is 121 cm². What is the perimeter of the square? _____

17. Convert the sum of 8659 m² and 37 426 m² to hectares. _____

18. A tank holds 360 litres when full. How many litres does the tank
contain when it is three-quarters full? _____

19. How many faces has each of these prisms?

(a) hexagonal prism _____ (b) triangular prism _____ (c) rectangular prism _____

20. Write one word to describe each angle below.

_____ _____ _____ _____ _____

Statistics and Probability

21. The 11 letters of the word MATHEMATICS were each written on separate cards. If the cards were
well shuffled, which letter or letters have the best chance of being drawn? _____

22. The ages of students on a bus are recorded in the table below.

Age	Students
13	5
14	7
15	11
16	12
17	6

What is the mode?

_____

Mutton Bird Isles

Bass Strait is a narrow grey ribbon of restless sea some three hundred kilometres wide that separates the huge land mass of Australia from its smaller shield-shaped island of Tasmania. It is well known to sailors as one of the wildest, most wicked stretches of water in the world, for numbers of islands surrounded by fierce rip tides, rocky shoals and shallows crouch in wait for unwary ships. Many have come to grief in this strait from either storms or from fog and their skeletons lie lost, forgotten, shrouded in kelp beneath the sullen depths.

Although Tasmania was first sighted by Abel Tasman, the Dutch explorer, in 1642, the Bass Strait islands remained undiscovered by Europeans until 1773 when Tobias Furneaux, aboard the Adventure became separated by fog from the Resolution and her captain, James Cook. The result was his discovery of a group of islands to the east of the Strait which now bear his name.

But it was the savage storm that wrecked the unseaworthy Sydney Cove on to Preservation Island in 1797 that really drew attention to the little-known area, for the ship carried a full cargo of rum from India. By the following year, the intrepid explorers Matthew Flinders and George Bass had made haste in the colonial sloop Norfolk to prove their theory that Tasmania was indeed divided from the rest of Australia by a strait. Their reports and the reports on the abundance of seals on the islands brought the first of the white settlers, many of them rough and ruthless men used to hard living. It was easy enough for them to steal Aboriginal women from nearby Tasmania and it was these men and women who were to become the ancestors of a unique group of islanders that still live on Cape Barren Island in the Furneaux Group.

The Strait offers ideal breeding conditions for the prolific bird life, particularly for the Short-tailed Shearwater, a member of the petrel family. Each spring, at the end of September, these birds of the ocean converge on the islands in their millions having completed a five-month migratory flight that has taken them on a figure-of-eight course across the wide wild expanse of the Pacific Ocean. These shearwaters, called Moonbirds by the Cape Barren Islanders, are more commonly known as Muttonbirds, a name originating from the days of the early sealers, who relied on them greatly to supplement their often dwindling food supplies. So regulated, so instinctive is the birds' return, that the Bass Strait islanders can almost set their clocks by them and the date on their calendars. They have reason to do so, for their arrival means a source of income.

Come late March, a strange thing happens. Small groups of islanders, particularly from Cape Barren Island, gather together to go 'birding', killing and processing for commercial gain thousands of young shearwaters, an occurrence that has taken place ever since the islands were settled. The toll, now carefully supervised and controlled by the Tasmanian National Parks and Wildlife Service, is said to be the greatest mass slaughter of birds in the world, yet it does no real harm to their numbers for many of the breeding colonies throughout the Strait are left unmolested.

From *Night of the Muttonbirds* by Mary Small

Reading and Comprehension

1. Why does the area have such a fearsome reputation?

(a) It is between the mainland and Tasmania.

(b) It was discovered by Abel Tasman.

(c) It has fierce tides and rocky shoals.

(d) It is shrouded in fog.

2. The islands in the east of Bass Strait were discovered by

(a) Abel Tasman.

(b) James Cook.

(c) Tobias Furneaux.

(d) George Bass and Matthew Flinders.

3. The first white settlers settled on the islands because of

(a) their remote location.

(b) the abundance of seals.

(c) the proximity to the mainland.

(d) the dangerous waters.

4. Which bird completes its five-month migratory flight at these islands?

_____

5. Though not stated, what inference can be taken from paragraph 3?

(a) It was essential to prove that Tasmania was separated from the rest of Australia.

(b) The white settlers made a living seal hunting.

(c) The *Sydney Cove* was wrecked on Preservation Island.

(d) both (a) and (b)

6. Why do you think the shearwaters were called muttonbirds?

_____

_____

Spelling and Vocabulary

Rewrite the misspelt words.

7. The islanders relyed on the birds to supplemant their food supplies.

_____

8. The harvesting of the muttonbirds is carefully supervised and controled.

_____

_____

Circle the word that has the nearest meaning to the underlined word.

9. The island is known for its <u>prolific</u> bird life.

(a) elegant

(b) prescribed

(c) abundant

(d) constant

10. These <u>intrepid</u> explorers set out from Western Port.

(a) wise

(b) carefree

(c) organised

(d) daring

Circle the correct word in brackets.

11. The (strait / straight) line was drawn between the two points.

12. The (coarse / course) the birds travelled never varied.

Grammar and Punctuation

13. Add another principal clause to this simple sentence.

Many of them wandered over the island

_____

_____

14. Punctuate and capitalise this text.

when do you expect to see them arrive asked don late evening next tuesday ill bet replied lauren

_____

_____

_____

_____

Number and Algebra

1. Plot these points on the number line below.
    (a) 30   (b) –65
    (c) 32 less than zero   (d) 15 more than –70

    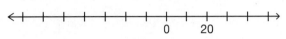

2. Use the appropriate signs (> or <) to make
    this statement true.

    $$36 \,\rule{1.5cm}{0.4pt}\, -4 \,\rule{1.5cm}{0.4pt}\, -26$$

3. (a) List the factors of 64.   _____
    (b) List the factors of 36.   _____
    (c) The common factors are   _____ .
    (d) The HCF of 64 and 36 is   _____ .

4. What number should be added to the
    sum of 3 tenths and 4 thousandths
    to equal 10?   _____

5. (a) Write the number which
        is one-hundredth of 4.3.   _____
    (b) Write the number which
        is one-thousandth of 0.7.   _____

6. (a) _____ $- 3794 = 5000 - 275$
    (b) $3000 \times$ _____ $= 270\,000$

7. Change the following fractions to decimal form.
    $\dfrac{11}{20}$ _____ $\dfrac{7}{50}$ _____ $\dfrac{19}{25}$ _____

8. $2\dfrac{7}{8}$ plus $3\dfrac{2}{3} =$ _____

9. What is 20% of $150?   _____

10. The ratio of cars to tyres is 1 to 4.
    If there are 12 cars, how many tyres
    are there?   _____

11. Simplify this algebraic expression.
    $\dfrac{24y}{9} =$ _____

12. If the length of one side of a square is
    $3x + 7$ cm, is the perimeter of that square
    $4 \times 3x + 7$, $4(3x + 7)$ or $\dfrac{3x}{4} + 7 \times 4$?
    Circle the correct one.

13. If $p = -3$, what is the value of p^2? _____

14. What is the product of
    $4ab$ and $2c$?   _____

Measurement and Space

15. A baker's shop prepared the following loaves
    of bread: forty 250-g loaves, eighty 350-g
    loaves and twenty-five 400-g loaves. How
    many kilograms of bread were baked?

    _____

16. 20 cm – 8 mm = _____ cm

17. What is the area of a parallelogram with a
    base of 14 cm and height of 9 cm?

    _____

18. From a vat containing 100 litres, a shopkeeper
    filled two and a half dozen 70-mL bottles.
    How much was left in the vat?   _____

19. Draw the vertical segment AB
    which is parallel to ray DC.

20. Name the following angles.

    (a) x and z are _____
        angles.
    (b) x and y are _____
        angles.
    (c) w is vertically opposite to _____ .

Statistics and Probability

21. A box contains 20 chocolates: 10 dark,
    5 milk, 3 white and 2 caramel.
    If a piece is taken at random, which one is
    least likely to be chosen?   _____

22. What is the mode of this
    set of scores?   _____
    16, 18, 14, 19, 23, 27, 14, 14, 19, 14

Stradbroke Island

… Suddenly a huge storm rose from the sea and the Noonuccal Tribe had to shelter as best they could.

When finally the storm moved away from the island, they gathered their hunting tools and food and went as fast as they could to the end of the island, worrying about the old woman they had tied to the stake.

When they arrived they were horrified to find the end of the island rock, where they had tied the old woman, had been cut away from the island by the electrical storm. They tried to reach her, but the winds were still howling and they could not. They tried throwing food to her but it fell down into the raging sea. The old woman was crying for them to help her, but there was nothing they could do to get to her. The winds howled for many days and many nights and finally the old woman died.

Now when the winds blow, all the Noonuccal Tribe can hear her death cries and the sea sends a spout of water high in the air to remind the Noonuccals of this terrible thing they did. All Noonuccals know that the punishment will always be with them, they will always hear her death cries and the sea will always send a huge spray of water high into the air to remind them.*

* There is a blowhole at the end of Minjerribah at Mooloomba (Point Lookout).
From *Legends of Our Land* by Oodgeroo Noonuccal

Reading and Comprehension

1. Why did the Noonuccal tribe return as fast as they could to the end of the island?
   (a) They were afraid of losing their tools.
   (b) There was another storm approaching.
   (c) They were worried about the old woman.
   (d) The winds were howling.

2. What will remind the tribe's children of the actions of their ancestors?
   (a) the howling winds
   (b) the death cries
   (c) the spray of water high in the air
   (d) all of the above

3. Find one point in the text which indicates that the Noonuccal tribe regret their treatment of the old woman.
   _____

4. What blocked the tribe from assisting the old woman?
   _____

5. Does the storyteller feel that the people should be ashamed of their actions? If so, explain.
   _____
   _____

6. What do you think is the purpose of the legend?
   _____

Spelling and Vocabulary

Rewrite the misspelt words.

7. They went to the northanmost part of the iland.
   _____

8. The trible elders were very angrey with her.
   _____

Circle the word that has the nearest meaning to the underlined word.

9. The rock <u>sheltered</u> the old woman.
   (a) shielded   (b) endangered
   (c) jeopardised   (d) exposed

10. Aboriginals have strong <u>ties</u> with their ancestors.
    (a) thoughts   (b) disunions   (c) links   (d) bonds

Circle the correct word in brackets.

11. The lady spoke with a foreign (ascent / accent).

12. Mum asked me to wind the (cord / chord) tightly around the handle.

Grammar and Punctuation

13. Underline the verbs in this sentence.
    'Stay there and growl to yourself,' the elders told the lady who was still complaining.

14. Punctuate and capitalise this sentence.
    wailing rock is where the old woman cried for help
    _____
    _____

Number and Algebra

1. Complete:

$x =$	1	2	3	4	5
$x^2 =$					
$x^3 =$					

2. $\sqrt{25} = 5$ and $\sqrt{36} = 6$
   What is $\sqrt{30}$ approximately? _____

3. Convert these fractions to decimals.
   Use your calculator.
   $\frac{17}{20}$ _____ $\frac{11}{40}$ _____ $\frac{27}{60}$ _____

4. Change $\frac{3}{125}$ to thousandths. _____
   Then write it as a decimal. _____

5. On a number line, movement to the right is
   movement in a _ _ _ _ _ _ _ _
   direction.

6. From the sum of 3796 and 11 211,
   subtract the difference between
   10 000 and 4289. _____

7. By how much is 29.029 greater
   than 14.374? _____

8. What is the difference between
   $7\frac{1}{2}$ and $1\frac{11}{16}$? _____

9. A purse contained $19.80. After 5% had been
   spent, how much remained? _____

10. Simplify the ratio $30:3$. _____

11. Which of these algebraic expressions will
    give the answer $a + b + c$?
    (a) $(a + b) + c$ (b) $a + (b + c)$
    (c) $(a + c) + b$ (d) any or all of these

12. Substitute known numbers ($a = 5$, $b = 2$)
    for the unknowns to prove that
    $5a - 3b + 4a$ equals $9a - 3b$. _____

13. Solve $13 - x = 7$. _____

14. How many days are in
    m weeks? _____

Measurement and Space

15. 750 g + 85 g = _____ kg = _____ t

16. One side of a scalene triangle is 32.7 cm.
    The second side is 60% larger than the first,
    whereas the third side is only 0.3 times the
    size of the second side. What is the
    perimeter of this shape? _____

17. What is the area of a triangle with base
    2.4 m and height 1.6 m? _____

18. A cube of granite has an edge of 206 mm.
    What is the volume of this shape in cm³?
    _____

19. Circle the octagon.

20. (a) Draw a diagram where ABC and CBD are
       complementary.

    (b) What type of angle is ABD?
    _____

Statistics and Probability

21. There are 100 tickets to be sold in an
    Easter Raffle. 5 tickets cost $1.
    What are my chances of winning
    first prize if I bought 5 tickets?
    _____

22. Here are 6 scores: 24, 18, 16, 19, 20, 10.
    What is the median? _____

How a newsreader looks

EH: What do you have to do to prepare yourself for going to air?

GD: Well ... you have to be made up.

EH: Does this take long?

GD: For a woman it takes about twenty to twenty-five minutes. Let's say half an hour with hair and make-up. For a man it takes about ten minutes. Men have make-up on but they usually don't have the eye make-up, they don't have the lipstick, they don't have anything like the effort put into shading on their cheekbones and that sort of thing. And of course their hair is usually much more basic than women's hair.

EH: Is it like stage make-up?

GD: No, it's not stage make-up exactly. In the old days of television the impression was that you had to be somewhat larger than life. Now we don't think that; we go for a much more natural look.

EH: But newsreaders dress well, don't they?

GD: I wish people were allowed to wear open-necked shirts and short sleeves, but in Australia it's been considered inappropriate. Actually the camera only sees the top half. We don't always take care with what we wear below the desk.

From *TV News* by Elizabeth Halley

Reading and Comprehension

1. How do newsreaders prepare to go to air?
   (a) have make-up applied   (b) get dressed
   (c) have hair styled   (d) all of the above

2. In the early days of television the emphasis was on making the newsreader
   (a) look natural.   (b) be larger than life.
   (c) wear a lot of make-up.   (d) both (b) and (c)

3. What is the difference between stage make-up and make-up for TV?

   _____

4. Which part of the newsreader's attire is least significant?

   _____

5. Which statement indicates that the interviewer believes that newsreaders should dress more casually?

   _____

6. Which of these statements is implied, but not stated?
   (a) Newsreaders are hilarious.
   (b) A male newsreader is easily prepared for the camera.
   (c) Australian newsreaders always dress in casual gear.
   (d) Blow-drying hair takes about 20 minutes.

Spelling and Vocabulary

Rewrite the misspelt words.

7. Who advisers you on how to dress?

   _____

8. There's tremondous competithon on television nowadays.

   _____

Circle the word that has the nearest meaning to the underlined word.

9. The athlete's will to win was <u>indomitable</u>.
   (a) feeble   (b) suppressible
   (c) preventable   (d) irrepressible

10. The toddler <u>tittered</u> at the sight of the clowns.
    (a) roared   (b) giggled
    (c) laughed loudly   (d) tired

Circle the correct word in brackets.

11. My dad's (vane / vain) about his appearance.

12. The actor walked (strait / straight) to her dressing room.

Grammar and Punctuation

13. Supply suitable adverbs.

    The newsreader read the words on the

    autocue _____ and _____ .

14. Punctuate and capitalise this sentence.

    what happens after youve had your hair and make-up done

    _____

    _____

Number and Algebra

1. Arrange this set in descending order.
   $0.8, 76\%, \frac{4}{6}, 0.099, \frac{4}{3}$

   _____

2. Complete.
   $997\,862 = 9 \times 10^5 +$ _____ $\times$ _____
   $+$ _____ $\times 10^3 +$ _____ $\times 10^\square +$
   $6 \times 10^\square +$ _____ $\times$ _____$^\square$

3. What is the place value of the seven in this number?
   five million, seven hundred and four thousand, three hundred and eight _____

4. Circle the greater fraction in each of these pairs.
   (a) $\frac{5}{9}, \frac{5}{6}$ (b) $\frac{7}{12}, \frac{16}{24}$ (c) $\frac{3}{4}, \frac{4}{5}$

5. $\frac{22}{7}$ (a) Is this rational or irrational? _____

   (b) Divide 22 by 7, writing your answer to the nearest ten-thousandth. _____

6. A machine planted 75 seedlings in each of 38 rows and 114 in another row.
   How many seedlings were planted altogether? _____

7. From the largest take the smallest:
   seventy-one tenths, ninety-seven thousandths and forty-seven hundredths _____

8. Subtract $1\frac{1}{10}$ from $5\frac{3}{5}$. _____

9. A test consisted of 40 questions. If Carla achieved a result of 80%, what was her score? _____

10. A book has 70 pages. Symon has read 40 pages. What is the ratio of pages read to total pages? _____

11. If 4 times a multiplied by b equals $4ab$, what is 6 times x multiplied by y? _____

12. Find the value of x: $\frac{x}{2} = 3.5$ _____

13. Expand $3(4 - a)$. _____

14. Laura has w golf balls and loses 2 balls. How many balls remain? _____

Measurement and Space

15. How many hours are there in 7 days and 8 hours? _____

16. An equilateral triangle has a perimeter of 4.8 cm. What is the length of each side?

    _____

17. A square has an area of 121 m². What length are its sides? _____

18. Which shape has the greater volume: a cube with a side of 11 cm or a rectangular prism with length 7 cm, width 4 cm and height 6 cm? _____

19. A cone has a curved _____ and a _____ . The point at the top is called a _____ . The net of the cone is a sector and a _____ .

20. How many degrees are there at the centre of a semicircle?

    _____

Statistics and Probability

21. What is the probability of drawing a green disc from a bag containing 10 black, 5 green, 3 red and 2 white discs?

    _____

22. Here are Owen's results in four tests.

    6   8 x 10

    If the mean result in the four tests was 7, what was his result in the third test? _____

An Australian UFO Mystery

An Australian UFO (unidentified flying object) sighting occurred in 1978. Frederick Valentich vanished without a trace over Bass Strait on 21 October that year.

Valentich, a twenty-year-old flying instructor, left Moorabbin, Victoria, in his Cessna 182 aircraft on a flight to King Island, Tasmania.

At 6:19 pm he reported sighting an unidentified aircraft to the Melbourne Flight Service Unit Controller.

He said he could not identify what type of aircraft was passing over him, at least 1000 feet (305 metres) above, except that it was very brightly lit and travelling at an 'unknown' speed.

The Unit Controller reported that there was no known air traffic in the vicinity.

Valentich then said the craft was orbiting on top of him, that it had a green light, and was 'sort of metallic and all shiny on the outside'.

He kept in contact with the Unit Controller for about six minutes, then all transmission ceased. His last words were, 'My intentions are to go to King Island … that strange aircraft is hovering on top of me again … it is hovering and it is not an aircraft.'

The weather in the Cape Otway area was clear. An intensive search was continued until 25 October, but no trace of the aircraft was found.

From *Strange Mysteries* by Rachael Collinson

Reading and Comprehension

1. An unidentified flying object is called that because
   (a) no-one knows what they are.
   (b) they are brightly lit.
   (c) their speed is unknown.
   (d) they are very big.

2. Flight controllers were unable to help Valentich because
   (a) he intended to go to King Island.
   (b) they couldn't verify the existence of a UFO.
   (c) he was flying a Cessna 182.
   (d) the UFO was so close to him.

3. Which Victorian town was Valentich's departure site?

4. Over which stretch of water did Valentich disappear?

5. In your opinion, would the prevailing weather conditions have helped or hindered Valentich's flight?

6. Which phrases used by the pilot indicate his difficulty in identifying the craft?

Spelling and Vocabulary

Rewrite the misspelt words.

7. I especialy liked reading this UFO mystry.

8. A UFO siteing was reported at a quartor to seven yesterday.

Circle the word that has the nearest meaning to the underlined word.

9. The <u>apparatus</u> that was used proved to be faulty.
   (a) obstruction   (b) impediment
   (c) instrument   (d) hindrance

10. He said he was <u>ostracised</u> from flying school last year.
    (a) welcomed   (b) banished
    (c) included   (d) oscillated

Circle the correct word in brackets.

11. Lucy's parental views are the (conserve / converse) of mine.

12. Many crystals and pearls were (sewn / sown) into the bride's (vail / veil).

Grammar and Punctuation

13. Circle the adverbial clause.

    The pilot could not identify the craft because it was too dark.

14. Punctuate and capitalise this sentence.

    at the last christmas concert jack played the part of santa claus in angels down under

Number and Algebra

1. Write the highest common factor for:
   (a) 24, 60 _____
   (b) 54, 81 _____

2. $24\,000\,000 + 700\,000 + 80\,000 + 80 + 4$
   = _____

3. Round 37.2479 to the nearest tenth _____
   hundredth _____
   thousandth _____

4. Reduce these fractions to lowest terms.
   (a) $\frac{45}{80}$ _____   (b) $\frac{21}{35}$ _____

5. Start at + 4. Go 5 places in the negative direction, then 3 in the positive direction. Where do you arrive? _____

   ```
   ‹─┬──┬──┬──┬──┬──┬──┬──┬──┬──┬──┬──┬──›
    -6 -5 -4 -3 -2 -1  0 +1 +2 +3 +4 +5 +6
   ```

6. A factory produces 3729 items per hour. How many items will be manufactured in 5 days of 8 hours each? _____

7. Use your calculator to find the number of packets of noodles at 85c each that could be bought with $56.95. _____

8. $7\frac{3}{4} - 5\frac{1}{6} =$ _____

9. The total enrolment at Dilston Primary School is 780 students. Last Friday 85% of the population was present. How many were absent? _____

10. Olivia bought a packet of 6 hot-cross buns. After two days, 4 of the buns have been eaten. What is the ratio of eaten buns to not eaten? _____

11. $2 + 5y = 27$
    What is the value of y? _____

12. If $3(x - 1) = 15$, what is the value of x? _____

13. Simplify $2p - 3p - 4p$. _____

14. If $a = 4$ and $b = -2$, what is the value of $3ab$? _____

Measurement and Space

15. Jalna has Saturday and Sunday off each week. If 1 August is a Wednesday, how many days will she work during that month? _____

16. The rectangular enclosure around a pool complex has a perimeter of 82 metres. It is 28 metres long. What is its area? _____

17. Eight fences are each 9.055 km long. What is the total length of the fencing? _____

18. What volume is equal to one-seventh of 12.32 litres? _____

19. Angles a and b are complementary; c and d are also complementary. If all four angles are adjacent, then a, b, c and d are _____.

20. What is the sum of these 4 angles?

_____

Statistics and Probability

21. The names of the months were written on cards and put in a box. What is the probability of drawing out a month that:
    (a) has 30 days? _____
    (b) begins with the letter M? _____
    (c) is the month before September? _____
    (d) is a summer month? _____

22. The minimum temperatures in Naracoorte over a week are recorded.

3 °C	-2 °C	1°C	7°C
2 °C	3 °C	-1 °C	

    What is the range of temperatures?

    _____

China's growing economy

The rise of the Chinese economy over the past three decades has greatly changed the global economic picture. China has a population of about 1 410 000 000. It has more people than the United States and Europe combined!

China boasts a trillion-dollar economy. But how has this miracle been achieved? New technologies have allowed more of the Chinese people to become efficient in the area of productivity. New machinery, better technology and more investment have helped raise the country's output.

It's quite simple. Market-orientated reforms have worked. The country's economic efficiency was raised by introducing 'profit incentives' for the rural sector, family farms, small private businesses, foreign investment and for trade. And, the planning was successful. Give the people 'a slice-of-the-action'.

The average household in China saves about 30 per cent of their income. That's a third! This enables a huge flow of the country's money to be circulated back through the core of China.

The country produces manufacturing goods that are consumed domestically but also exported. China is recognised as a bit of an 'innovator' when it comes to producing goods. It's a clever approach: produce goods that are cheap but also provide quality expensive goods as well. How many times have you seen the label 'Made in China'?

Reading and Comprehension

1. China has a population of about
   - (a) 1.4 million.
   - (b) 1 million.
   - (c) 1.4 billion.
   - (d) 2 billion.

2. *30 per cent* represents
   - (a) productivity profit per annum.
   - (b) average household saving.
   - (c) the government's innovative expenditure.
   - (d) the economy's benchmark three decades ago.

3. Which one doesn't belong? An *innovation* is a
   - (a) change.
   - (b) modernism.
   - (c) novelty.
   - (d) suggestion.

4. Which word in the text refers to the countryside?

   _____

5. Which groups of people are the profit incentives geared towards?

   _____

6. Explain what the main idea is behind the market-orientated reforms.

   _____

Spelling and Vocabulary

Rewrite the misspelt words.

7. The gratest problem during the 1930s was unemploymant.

   _____

8. Men colapsed from hungar and exhauston.

   _____

Circle the word that has the nearest meaning to the underlined word.

9. Mrs Tedison dismissed us at 3 o'clock.
   - (a) released
   - (b) detained
   - (c) recalled
   - (d) jarred

10. Have a prosperous New Year!
    - (a) needy
    - (b) propounded
    - (c) wealthy
    - (d) profound

Circle the correct word in brackets.

11. The costume was too (shear / sheer).

12. Michaela kept (stairing / staring) into space!

Grammar and Punctuation

13. Add an *ing* verb form.

    Young Tabitha hates _____.

14. Punctuate and capitalise this sentence.

    brisbane born sue maylee has become the first australian to win a british amateur title in darts

    _____

    _____

    _____

Number and Algebra

1. Write the number for

   $11 + \frac{11}{10} + \frac{11}{100} + \frac{11}{1000}$: _____

2. When −192 is divided by 6 the result is:

   (a) 32   (b) 32−   (c) −32   (d) plus 32

3. Circle the number that (when rounded to the nearest hundredth) is thirty-two and fourteen hundredths.

   (a) 32.414   (b) 32 147 thousandths

   (c) 32.137

4. Are these two fractions equivalent?

   $\frac{3}{4}, \frac{12}{16}$ ☐ Yes   ☐ No

5. On a number line start at 0 then follow these movements: +3, −5, +7, −4.
   Where do you end up? _____

6. Use your calculator to find the answer to this number sentence.

   $(8735 \div 25) \times 18$ _____

7. By how much is 17.3715 less than fifty ones and 17 thousandths? _____

8. What is the product of $\frac{2}{3}$ and $\frac{9}{10}$? _____

9. The price of a TV is $1500. It is discounted by 10%. What is the new price of the TV?

   _____

10. Share 98 comics between two children in the ratio 3 to 4. _____

11. Which formula of perimeter of a plane shape can be expressed as $P = 4s$? _____

12. Points A, B, C and D have been plotted on the cartesian plane.

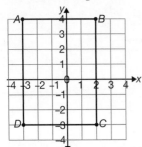

What is the area of the rectangle $ABCD$? _____

13. Could the formula for perimeter of a triangle be expressed as $P = a + b + c$? _____

14. What is the missing length? _____

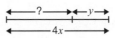

Measurement and Space

15. A clock started at 8:52 am and stopped at 9:17 am. Was it working for more or less than half an hour? _____

16. Find the perimeter of the trapezium.

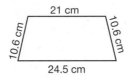

   _____

17. A rectangle has an area of 1080 m² and a breadth of 24 m. What is its length? _____

18. What is the difference between 3750 millilitres and 3.75 L? _____

19. Arrange 5 points so that there are three points in each of two line segments.

20. Name all of the angles that have X as a vertex.

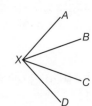

   _____, _____,

   _____, _____,

   _____,

Statistics and Probability

21. There are 9 discs in a hat: 4 red, 2 green, 2 yellow and 1 blue. What are the chances of taking out a yellow disc? _____

22. Here is a dot plot of 12 scores.

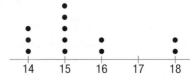

   Find: (a) mode _____

          (b) median _____

Why play sport?

Australia has a good climate for outdoor sports and lots of space for courts, pools, gymnasiums, ovals and other sporting complexes.

On Saturday or Sunday afternoons, places like beaches, bowling greens, race courses, golf courses, stadiums and tennis courts are crowded with both players and spectators.

People participate in sport for a variety of reasons. For example, there is something special about being part of a team. It encourages co-operation and brings people together. Team spirit develops as each team member works for the benefit of the group. Friendships are formed that can last for a lifetime.

Individual sportspeople strive for their best efforts by themselves. They must be self-motivated, disciplined and confident if they are to succeed in their chosen sport. They must also learn to accept both praise and criticism as well as success and defeat.

Sport is an adventure that provides entertainment for players and spectators alike. Australians play it and watch it with a passion and enthusiasm that no-one can beat!

From Sport in the Making by Shane Power

Reading and Comprehension

1. How can sport help us develop personally?
    (a) by encouraging co-operation among people
    (b) by disciplining others in the team
    (c) by teaching us to accept praise and success
    (d) by making us go to the beach on weekends

2. Individual sportspeople must
    (a) develop team spirit.
    (b) accept defeat and praise.
    (c) form friendships quickly to be part of a team.
    (d) both (a) and (b)

3. Which phrase means 'with an intense feeling'?
    _____

4. Australians are dispassionate about sport.
    True or false? _____

5. Why do you think people participate in sport?
    Give two reasons.
    _____
    _____

6. Which of these statements are implied but not stated?
    (a) Team spirit develops co-operation.
    (b) Team spirit develops a person's ability to work co-operatively in the workplace.
    (c) Team spirit develops so that sportspeople can accept praise and defeat.

Spelling and Vocabulary

Rewrite the misspelt words.

7. My favorite sports entertainment is hockey.
    _____

8. In Novembor she visited her reletives.
    _____

Circle the word that has the nearest meaning to the underlined word.

9. Today is a <u>dismal</u> day for swimming.
    (a) dim   (b) bleak
    (c) cheerful   (d) joyous

10. She has an <u>exceptional</u> butterfly stroke.
    (a) general   (b) superior
    (c) individual   (d) common

Circle the correct word in brackets.

11. Omar failed his driving test because he could not perform a (reserve / reverse) park.

12. Her (presents / presence) at the meeting was unexpected.

Grammar and Punctuation

13. Circle the phrases containing prepositions.
    In this weather, about the only thing one can do is sleep in a hammock.

14. Punctuate and capitalise this sentence.
    the diamonds won the netball world cup in 2023
    _____
    _____
    _____

Number and Algebra

1. What number is 16 times smaller than negative nineteen? _____

2. Can an irrational number be plotted exactly on a number line? ☐ Yes ☐ No

3. Complete the following:
    $15^2 =$ _____ $6^2 + 6^3 =$ _____

4. (a) $\frac{3}{8} + \frac{2}{5} =$ _____ + _____ = _____

    (b) $\frac{2}{3} - \frac{1}{5} =$ _____ − _____ = _____

5. Write these integers in order from smallest to largest: +3, +7, −6, −1, −5

    _____

6. A number multiplied by 69 gives a product of 5382. How much greater would the product be if the number was multiplied by 79? _____

7. Subtract 7.019 from 12. _____

8. Which of these operations result in a recurring decimal in the answer? Circle them.

    $427 \div 11$ $528 \div 12$ $616 \div 9$

9. A sales agent had to travel a distance of 280 km. After she has covered 55% of the distance, how far does she still have to travel? _____

10. In a box there are 12 red balls and 6 green balls. What is the ratio of green balls to red balls? _____

11. $b^2 \times c^3 \times d^4$ can be rewritten as

    _____ × _____ × _____ × _____
    × _____ × _____ × _____
    × _____ × _____

12. $x = 4(a + b)$ is the same as $x = 4a + b$, $x = 4a \times 4b$, $x = 4a + 4b$ or $a \times 4 \times b \times 4$. Circle the correct one.

13. What is the value of x?
    $2x + 11 = 21$ _____

14. What is the area of triangle XYZ? _____

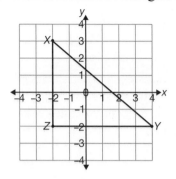

Measurement and Space

15. Last year Mia's school was opened for 202 days. If she attended 197 days, for how many days was she absent? _____

16. Choose the correct operation to convert m to km. We need to (× or ÷) by 1000. _____

17. A sheet of metal is 21 cm square. The sheet is bent to form a cylinder. What is the area of the curved surface of the outside of the cylinder? _____

18. Pour 3120 mL into these two containers in the given ratio.

    Can A will have _____ litres more than Can B.

19. A polygon with 5 equal sides is called a

    _ _ _ u _ _ _ _   _ _ _ t _ _ _ _ _ .

20. Colour in the vertically opposite angle of the shaded angle given.

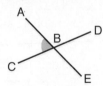

Statistics and Probability

21. Finish labelling the spinner so that A and B have the same chance and C is most likely.

22. In five soccer matches, Todd's team scored 4 goals in one game, 3 goals in 2 games and no goals in the rest of the games. What was the mean number of goals scored per game? _____

Widening options

A seemingly straightforward question often asked of young people is 'What do you want to be when you grow up?' For young people, choosing a future career is one of the biggest life decisions they will need to make. The response given is often based along gender lines with girls choosing hairdressing, nursing, teaching and other caring careers while boys respond with firefighting, engineering, construction and professional sports. Society's beliefs and perceptions of male or female gendered occupations strongly influence an individual's career aspirations and decisions.

While individual decisions may seem personal they also affect the nation's overall economic growth. Concern about Australia's performance in Science, Technology, Engineering and Mathematics (STEM) subjects and the take-up of STEM careers has resulted in the promotion of study choices made by students through the *National STEM School Education Strategy* (Education Council, 2015). The program is currently being implemented.

Many schools, at all levels, now promote STEM subjects and offer special enrichment programs in these areas. Sometimes these programs are conducted by regional Science and Technology centres, often with the support of local industries or service clubs. Many of these programs are aimed specifically at encouraging girls to engage with STEM subjects at school as, historically, these areas have been male dominated. Girls are also encouraged to follow through to future learning and work opportunities by participating in work experience, mentor programs, scholarships and other networking opportunities.

Participation in STEM education broadens the options and experiences of all students and supports them in choosing careers that will not only contribute to building a more prosperous nation and an inclusive scientific community but also will allow them to fulfil their potential.

Reading and Comprehension

1. STEM education is important because
   (a) young people do not know what career to choose.
   (b) scholarships will be available.
   (c) our nation will become more prosperous.
   (d) a national strategy has been developed.

2. Why do schools promote STEM subjects for girls?
   (a) to help them achieve higher scores at school
   (b) to broaden their future study and career options
   (c) to encourage them to become firefighters
   (d) to help them become members of the Education Council

3. What does mentoring mean?

   _____

4. Why is it important for boys and girls to have career choices?

   _____

5. Why do you think the *National STEM School Education Strategy* has been developed?

   _____

6. What jobs might become options for girls?

   _____

Spelling and Vocabulary

Rewrite the misspelt words.

7. Girls are encoureged to widen learning and work opportunities.

   _____

8. Sceince and Technology Centers promote STEM.

   _____

Circle the word that has the nearest meaning to the underlined word.

9. I sought solace by eating the chocolate bar.
   (a) discomfort (b) torment (c) solitude (d) comfort

10. The toddler stood there, grubby and unclad.
    (a) bare   (b) headstrong
    (c) wailing   (d) saturated

Circle the correct word in brackets.

11. The courageous knight said he would (caught / court) the princess.

12. Many of the (patience / patients) were in the waiting room.

Grammar and Punctuation

13. Insert a phrase containing an **adjective** in each sentence.
    (a) Tim liked the movie at _____ .
    (b) The cow with _____ had four calves.

14. Punctuate and capitalise this text.

    congratulations you got the job you start on monday good luck said the employer

    _____

    _____

Number and Algebra

1. Which is greater: 2^8 or 8^2? _____
   And by how much? _____

2. $2^2 \times 2^3 = ($ ____ $\times$ ____ $) \times (2 \times$ ____ $\times$ ____ $)$
   = ____ $\times$ ____ $\times$ ____ $\times$ ____
   $\times$ ____
   = $2^\square$

3. Round 0.1466 to the
   nearest thousandth. _____

4. Reduce each fraction to its lowest terms.
   (a) $\frac{9}{24}$ _____   (b) $\frac{20}{55}$ _____

5. (a) Simplify $374.85 \div 9 + (23.021 \times 4)$.

   _____

   (b) Arrange these in descending order.
   0.5, 0.56, 0.005, 0.006, 0.056

   _____

6. If Carla earns \$57 746 per year (52 weeks),
   what does she earn each week?
   Use your calculator. _____

7. The distance between two posts is 5.126 km.
   After Mia walked 3.278 km from the first
   post, how far does she need to walk to reach
   the second? _____

8. What is the quotient of 6 and $\frac{1}{8}$? _____

9. A firm ordered 140% of 150 tonnes
   of top soil. What was the total order
   in tonnes? _____

10. Simplify the ratio $2 : 4 : 10$. _____

11. Three people rewrote the equation
    $x \div y \times z$.
    (a) $\frac{x}{y} \times z$ (b) $\frac{xz}{y}$ (c) $\frac{x}{yxz}$
    Use substitution to prove which are correct.
    Circle only the correct ones.

12. a times the sum of x and y can be written as
    _____ .

13. $3x - 4 - 2x + 5 =$ _____

14. Complete the table using the rule $y = 6 - 2x$.

x	0	1	2	3
y				

Measurement and Space

15. Rewrite 7 kg 800 g in grams. _____

16. An equilateral triangle has a perimeter
    of 29.25 metres.
    How long is each side? _____

17. A triangle has a base of 45 mm and
    a perpendicular height of 32 mm.
    What is its area? _____

18. $387 \text{ L} + 143 \text{ L} =$ _____ L

19. A 'STOP' sign is commonly seen on the
    road. What shape is the sign?

    _____

20. Line segments AB and CD intersect at X.
    Name the reflex angles formed.

    _____

Statistics and Probability

21. A pack of cards contains 52 cards. What is
    the chance of selecting a queen at random?

    _____

22. The stem-and-leaf plot shows the ages of
    entrants in a fun run.

Stem	Leaf
3	29
4	0468
5	3359
6	1

   What is the mode? _____

The news at seven

Growing up, 7 pm each evening was significant —all work/play/noise ceased and the radio became the centre of family activity. The 7-pm time signal prompted the checking of clocks and the ABC's nightly national news bulletin took centre stage, providing a trusted source of news and information. Authoritative and well-modulated male voices presented local and national news while, later, overseas correspondents provided on-the-spot reports of international events.

With the advent of television, alliance shifted to the nightly 7 o'clock television news. News items were illustrated with video footage and reports from local journalists. Sometimes disturbing images were seen. Newsreaders, both male and female, became familiar faces and voices, welcomed into the home each day as reliable sources of the news.

Commercial radio stations and later television stations offered their own news services from 6 pm but in our home the ABC service reigned. Commercial news was often more dramatic, highlighting sometimes sensationalist happenings including crime. Stories from various news agencies provided an international flavour. Their presenters, too, became household names.

With the advent of 24-hour digital news services people are able to access the news at any time of the day and on a variety of platforms. Programming includes live news bulletins, repeats of other news or current-affairs programs, outside broadcasts, weather and sports reports. Instantaneous 'breaking news' bulletins from across the world provide repeated information and footage about an event as it unfolds.

'News Breakfast' now begins our day by providing updates on overnight events or follow-up on earlier items and the 7-pm evening bulletin allows us to sit back, catch up on missed news and reflect on the day's happenings.

Reading and Comprehension

1. Where do ABC news programs source their information?

   (a) local reporters

   (b) overseas correspondents

   (c) commercial radio and television stations

   (d) both (a) and (b)

2. What do 24-hour news services allow listeners and viewers to do?

_____

3. What is meant by the phrase 'well-modulated'?

_____

4. What is the purpose of overseas correspondents?

_____

5. Who are welcomed into homes each day?

_____

6. Why does the writer believe the ABC news is a trusted source of information?

_____

Spelling and Vocabulary

Rewrite the misspelt words.

7. Oversees correspondents provide reports of internashonal events.

_____

8. We can view mist news on digital services.

_____

Circle the word that has the nearest meaning to the underlined word.

9. The defeated army <u>abandoned</u> any hope of conquering their enemy.

   (a) defended   (b) supported

   (c) discarded   (d) upheld

10. He told us the story in <u>explicit</u> detail.

   (a) vague (b) obscure (c) specific (d) ambiguous

Circle the correct word in brackets.

11. It was a (shear / sheer) waste.

12. Her riding (breeches / breaches) had shrunk.

Grammar and Punctuation

13. Underline the **nouns**.

He is surrounded by people from different walks of life.

14. Punctuate and capitalise this sentence.

uncle georgio and aunty maria who live in greece have sent me a postcard of the acropolis

_____

_____

Number and Algebra

1. What is $1^3 + 2^2 + 3^1$? _____

2. Which number is two hundred thousand less than 48 934 182? _____

3. Continue halving until the lowest possible whole number is obtained.
   (a) 864 _____
   (b) 1440 _____

4. $\frac{2}{3} + \frac{2}{4} + \frac{2}{8} = \frac{6}{15}$
   Show the working that proves this answer is not correct.

   _____

5. Ground level in a building is floor 0. There are three basement carparks below and eight floors above the ground floor. What is the total number of floors? _____

6. Which of the following numbers are divisible by 5, 10 and 25?
   375, 1300, 1257 _____

7. $0.076 + 8.39 + 0.004 =$ _____

8. Find $\frac{4}{9} \times 261$ L. _____

9. What is 9% of 753 metres of calico? _____

10. Share a $40 prize in the ratio of $2 : 3$.

    _____

11. By the Distributive Law $x(a + b + c)$ is the same as _____ + _____ + _____.

12. Is $2a^2$ the same value as $(2a)^2$? Show by substitution to prove or disprove your answer.
    Prove _____ Disprove _____

13. What is the rule for this table of values? _____

x	−1	0	1	2	3
y	−2	−1	0	1	2

14. Use the cartesian plane to plot the points from the table in question 13.

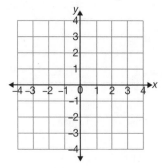

Measurement and Space

15. How many cans of soup weighing 0.4 kg each are in a group weighing 2.4 kg? _____

16. A length of wire is $42p$ cm. Olivia cuts the wire into 3 equal pieces. What is the length of each small piece? _____

17. What is the area of a triangular garden if the base measures 21 m and the shortest distance from the apex to the base is 18 m? _____

18. One container holds 3.25 litres and 4.16 litres are added to it. Another container holds 4.5 litres and 1.57 litres are removed. Which container now holds more and by how much? _____

19. How many interior angles does a regular octagon have? _____

20. If the measure of angle ABC is 70°, what is the measure of angle BCD?

    _____

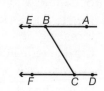

Statistics and Probability

21. The faces of a cube are painted as follows: 2 black, 2 red and 2 white. What is the probability of rolling a red face? _____

22. In a diving competition the five judges awarded the following scores:

    6.8   7.1   6.5   6.9   7.4

    What was the:
    (a) median? _____
    (b) mean? _____

Framing Ned Kelly

Sidney Nolan was born on 22 April 1917 at Carlton, Victoria. His parents were living in a town called Ngambie, in north-eastern Victoria, before he was born. This area is known as 'Kelly country' because Ned Kelly and his gang lived and roamed through it in the 1870s.

Soon after Sidney was born, he and his parents moved to a bayside Melbourne suburb called St Kilda. When Sidney became an artist, St Kilda often appeared in his paintings.

St Kilda was a lively place in the summer; crowded with holiday-makers. However, in the winter it was cold, bleak and eerily empty.

Sidney's father became a tram driver in Melbourne. He sometimes arranged for Sidney to travel on the tram for free. As a result, Sidney saw a lot of the city. Mr Nolan was also a keen member of the Tramways Lifesaving Club. Sidney used to accompany his father to the St Kilda pool each Sunday during the summer.

Sidney's mother loved going to the cinema and, much to the dismay of Sidney's school, would keep him home with her every Friday so that he could accompany her.

From *Framing Ned Kelly* by Louise Martin-Chew

Reading and Comprehension

1. According to the text what often appeared in Sidney Nolan's paintings?
   (a) Ngambie
   (b) the Tramways Lifesaving Club
   (c) St Kilda
   (d) Kelly country

2. What is St Kilda?
   (a) a town in south-east Victoria
   (b) a landmark
   (c) a bayside suburb
   (d) a Life Saving Club

3. Name the area in which Sidney Nolan was born.

   _____

4. In which century did the Kelly Gang live in Ngambie?

   _____

5. Why did Sidney's school react with dismay?

   _____

6. How do you think Nolan's experiences as a youth helped him as an artist later in life?

   _____

   _____

Spelling and Vocabulary

Rewrite the misspelt words.

7. He compleated many paintings during the war years.

   _____

8. Nolan finished a serries of Ned Kelly picturs.

   _____

Circle the word that has the nearest meaning to the underlined word.

9. This contract is now underlined{terminated}.
   (a) started   (b) established
   (c) concluded   (d) initiated

10. The Board of Directors vacillated before they reached their final decision.
    (a) investigated   (b) fluctuated
    (c) verified   (d) checked

Circle the correct word in brackets.

11. They (sort / sought) relief from the burning sun.

12. The salesman found a strong (ally / alley) in his boss.

Grammar and Punctuation

13. Underline the clause containing a noun.

    'Is this right?' asked Grandma Jill.

14. Punctuate and capitalise this text.

    some nsw candidates belong to no political party at all are they called independents

    _____

    _____

Mathematics

Number and Algebra

1. (a) Write 1 460 037 in expanded notation.

_____

   (b) Write 8 700 903 in exponential notation.

_____

2. Expand 12 813 643.5 _____

_____

3. Convert each common fraction to a decimal fraction.

   (a) $\frac{4}{5}$ _____   (b) $\frac{1}{3}$ _____   (c) $\frac{3}{4}$ _____   (d) $\frac{4}{50}$ _____   (e) $\frac{6}{8}$ _____

4. Make each number 1000 times smaller.

   (a) 268 _____   (b) 1358 _____   (c) 97 _____   (d) 9 _____

5. Write the answer in the box.

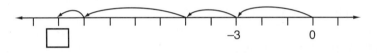

6. What is the difference between these two number sentences? _____

   $(15 \times 6) \times 3 =$ _____ $15 \times (6 \times 3) =$ _____

7. (a)   12.5
         × 60
       _____

       _____

   (b)   1.01
         × 0.1
       _____

       _____

   (c)   5.098
         × 43
       _____

       _____

       _____

8. Multiply $\frac{3}{8}$ by $\frac{1}{2}$ _____

9. Shade in 60% of this shape.

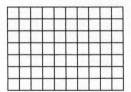

10. What is the ratio of 14 days to 3 weeks?

_____

11. If y has a value of 3, then what is the value of this algebraic expression?

    $5(y + y^2 + y^3) =$ _____

12. The perimeter of a square is $3x$. The length of one side of this square is _____ .

13. Solve the equation $3a - 5 = 16$.   _____

14. Simplify $4b + 2b^2 - 3b + b^2$.   _____

Answers

UNIT **1** page 8

Maths

1. one hundred and seventy-five million, seven hundred and fifty thousand
2. 9, 10, 11, 12, 13, 14, 15, 16
3. 1, 2, 3, ④, 5, ⑥, 7, ⑧, ⑨ 0
4. $\frac{1}{20}, \frac{1}{5}, \frac{1}{4}, \frac{3}{10}, \frac{1}{2}$
5. 7.77   6. 2 860 000
7. 13.404
8. (a) $5\frac{1}{2}$ (b) $3\frac{3}{8}$
9. $52   10. 1 : 100
11. $a + b$
12. (a) 8   (b) 8
13. $12xy$
14.

x	0	1	2	3
y	1	3	5	7

15. 9 h 25 min
16. 16×87 mm = 1.392 m
17. 276 m² less than 1 ha
18. 2 cm
19. Suggested answers:
20. 65°; 75°; 40°
21. 5 outcomes   22. 11

English

1. d   2. c
3. An animal which has a pouch to hold its young.
4. They destroy pastures for sheep; knock down fences; dig holes that break animals' legs.
5. Suggested answer: Because females might be pregnant, killing a female animal could cause population problems in the long term.
6. Suggested answers: No, he is very defensive; he asks for understanding; he tries to justify why he kills wombats.
7. Break, their
8. don't   9. a
10. d
11. fur
12. can't
13. Here is the wombat which destroyed my fences.
14. I shot the wombat. Why not?

UNIT **2** page 10

Maths

1. 133
2. 409.377
3. (a) 8, 16, 24, 32, 40
   (b) 12, 24, 36, 48, 60
   (c) 24
   (d) 24
4. $3\frac{15}{100}$ $\left(3\frac{3}{20}\right)$
5.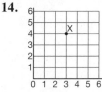
6. 6.228
7. 2.355
8. $5\frac{7}{10}$
9. $12.90
10. 1 : 6
11. $4x - 3$
12. 39
13. $2a + 3b$
14.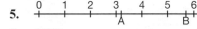
15. 11:09 am
16. 16 lengths
17. 23 000 cm²; 2 300 000 mm²
18. 6.028 568 m³
19. perpendicular
20. 37°
21. $\frac{1}{6}$
22. 17

English

1. c   2. b
3. It refers to his toy-delivering flight on Xmas Eve.
4. about a week
5. [2], [4], [1], [3]
6. c
7. Excess, disappeared
8. suit
9. b
10. b
11. coral
12. frieze
13. fungus; terminus
14. Santa had to run, jog, skip, row and diet till Christmas Day.

UNIT **3** page 12

Maths

1. 583.714
2. >
3. 47.09
4. $\frac{1}{4}, \frac{1}{3}, \frac{3}{8}, \frac{17}{24}, \frac{5}{6}$
5. –2
6. 40 251
7. 11.48
8. $88.35
9. 2108 sheep
10. 7 : 3
11. $3 \times 3 (3 + 5)$
    $= 3 \times 3 \times 3 + 15 \times 3 = 72$
12. $y = 5$
13. $2x + 4y$
14. $5p + 2q$
15. 7:35; 1935
16. 23 cm
17. 84.64 m²
18. 32 cm³
19. 1
20. Parent/teacher to check; $\angle EDC$
21. 1 chance out of 6 $\left(\frac{1}{6}\right)$
22. 54

English

1. a
2. b
3. He was the head astronomer.
4. a buy now, pay later arrangement
5. 160 rupees
6. Suggested answer: because it was an everyday example the students would understand
7. two
8. scent
9. d
10. c
11. sent
12. advice
13. Suggested answers:
    (a) Louise strolled through the park and picked the flowers.
    (b) Gordon will run here to get fit.
14. That's positive. That's negative.
    or
    That's positive; that's negative.

Answers

UNIT **4** page 14

Maths

1. 3000, 100, 20, 1
   3000, 100, 20, 1 = 3121
2. two million, four hundred and eighty-three thousand and six
3. 45
4. $(3 \times 5) \times 8 + 7^2 - 9 \div 3 = 166$
5. +5
6. 301 990
7. 64.215
8. (a) $1\frac{1}{6}$ (b) $9\frac{3}{8}$
9. 2 220 000 kg
10. 15
11. $(5 + 7) + 9 = 5 + (7 + 9)$
    $12 + 9 = 5 + 16$
    $21 = 21$ true
12. $\frac{b^2}{10\,000}$
13. $m = 5$
14. $10n$ km
15. 34.16 t
16. $(7x + 5y)$ cm
17. 216 cm², 108 cm² (half)
18. 18 L
19. 8 faces
20. $\angle b = 38°$, $\angle c = 90°$
21. $\frac{3}{8}$
22. 3

English

1. d
2. a
3. Body Focus
4. one month's trial
5. Suggested answer: Yes—he is worried about how his body looks.
6. d, a, c, b
7. neighbours, champions
8. thankful, ordeal
9. a
10. d
11. profit
12. tract
13. (a) happiness (b) freedom
14. 'Well,' said our aerobics teacher, 'who's ready for some cardiovascular training?'

UNIT **5** page 16

Maths

1. 6, 22, 33, 46, 78
2. 5 000 361 400
3. 38.111, 38.101, 38.011, 38.01, 38.001
4. Suggested answers: $\frac{12}{50}$, $\frac{6}{25}$
5. 8
6. A = 24, B = 12, C = 15
7. 9.133
8. $8\frac{9}{16}$
9. $1650
10. 9
11. false
12. $3x$
13. (3, 2)
14. 12
15. 185 g
16. 195.8 cm
17. 6.25 cm
18. 294.84 cm³
19. A square pyramid has an apex and one less face. Four of the faces are triangular—in a prism they are all squares/rectangles.
20. 50°
21. 16 outcomes
22. 80

English

1. c
2. c
3. Elvin Industries
4. playground
5. Suggested answer: Because it recognises achievement and encourages others to achieve their best.
6. d, c, a, b
7. career, politics
8. carried, thorough, research
9. d
10. c
11. purposely
12. further
13. active
14. To my utter dismay, Councillor Jones won the seat of Griffiths again.

UNIT **6** page 18

Maths

1. (a) $2 \times 2 \times 2 \times 2 \times 2 \times 2$
   (b) 8^2
2. $-7, -5.2, -2.3, 47\%, 2\frac{1}{4}, 5.75$
3. 0.8
4. (a) 3.16 (b) 15.8
5. (a) 11.473 (b) 72.115
6. 67 7. 4.98
8. $4\frac{3}{16}$
9. 0.23, 0.17, 0.04
10. 18
11. $5 \times a + 5 \times b = 5a + 5b$
12. 15 13. a
14.

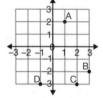

15. 65 kg 0 g
16. 420
17. 10 mm
    10 mm × 10 mm = 100 mm²
    10 mm × 10 mm × 10 mm = 1000 mm³
18. same volume
19. True
20. $\angle TOB$ and $\angle BOT$
21. 1 out of 26 22. 3

English

1. d 2. d
3. He could spin a yarn like no-one else.
4. good day
5. Suggested answers: happy, good hearted, imaginative, kind
6. the last paragraph (weight of flies)
7. welcoming
8. sheer, weight
9. c 10. d
11. through
12. were
13. Suggested answer: The sheep was shorn.
14. Billy said, 'The mozzies settled down in a swamp to snooze through the day's heat.'

Answers

Maths

1. (a) $300\,000 + 7000 + 900 + 4$
   (b) $5 \times 10^5 + 2 \times 10^4 + 4 \times 10^3 + 8 \times 10^0$
2. $10, \dfrac{7}{10}, \dfrac{2}{100}, \dfrac{5}{1000}$
3. 3969, 2023, 6923
4. (a) 26.1   (b) 5.39
5. $+6, +3, -2, -8$
6. 49 680   7. 9.198
8. $5\dfrac{5}{12}$ 9. $1235.81
10. $5:6$
11. $3(3 \times 2 + 2^2) + 2 = 32$
12. 7   13. $2a - 10$
14.

15. 12:06 pm   16. 4.95 cm
17. 4 872 960 m², 487.296 ha
18. 14.750 L
19. square-based pyramid
20. (a) f (b) supplementary angles
21. $\dfrac{4}{8}$ (50%)   22. 16

English

1. a   2. b
3. Secretary of the Immigration Department (1951)
4. Conventions
5. Suggested answers: the goal of having a united national culture; the ideal of building supportive communities.
6. Suggested answers: to help them assimilate more easily into Australia; to have a uniform culture.
7. multicultural, equator
8. Migrants, adjusted
9. b   10. c   11. I
12. allowed, aisle
13. shortage; interpreters; levels; movement
14. Government services had to cater for non–English speaking migrants.

Maths

1. 215, 230, 245, 260, 275, 290
2. 15, 18, 21, 27, 42, 69, 111, 135
3. 10.5, 9, 7.5, 6, 4.5, 3, 1.5
4. $\dfrac{5}{6}, \dfrac{11}{15}, \dfrac{16}{30}, \dfrac{1}{2}, \dfrac{2}{5}$
5. Parent/teacher to check; -58
6. 328 m
7. $147.80
8. $4\dfrac{10}{21}$
9. 154 g
10. A
11. $\dfrac{xy}{z}$
12. $20x + 9y$
13. 5 and -5
14. $(1, 4), (1, -2), (4, -2)$
15. 72 kg 0 g
16. 44 cm
17. 4.6085 ha
18. 270 L
19. (a) 8   (b) 5   (c) 6
20. (a) acute   (b) obtuse
    (c) straight   (d) reflex
    (e) right
21. M, A or T
22. 16

English

1. c   2. c   3. b
4. Short-tailed Shearwater
5. d
6. Suggested answers: because they tasted like mutton (sheep); they could be cooked like mutton; the cooked bird looked or stayed fresh like mutton.
7. relied, supplement
8. carefully, controlled
9. c   10. d
11. straight   12. course
13. Suggested answer: Many of them wandered over the island and marvelled at the view.
14. 'When do you expect to see them arrive?' asked Don. 'Late evening next Tuesday, I'll bet,' replied Lauren.

Maths

1.
2. $36 > -4 > -26$
3. (a) 1, 2, 4, 8, 16, 32, 64
   (b) 1, 2, 3, 4, 6, 9, 12, 18, 36
   (c) 1, 2, 4   (d) 4
4. 9.696
5. (a) 0.043   (b) 0.0007
6. (a) 8519   (b) 90
7. 0.55, 0.14, 0.76
8. $6\dfrac{13}{24}$ 9. $30
10. 48   11. $\dfrac{8y}{3}$
12. $4(3x + 7)$
13. 9
14. $8abc$
15. 48 kg
16. 19.2 cm
17. 126 cm²
18. 79 litres
19. Parent/teacher to check
20. (a) vertically opposite
    (b) supplementary
    (c) y
21. caramel
22. 14

English

1. c   2. d
3. They hurried back to find her; they were horrified when they saw the rock was cut off.
4. The rock had been cut away by the storm; the winds blew away food.
5. Yes; the use of phrases: 'terrible thing they did' and 'the punishment will always be with them'.
6. to explain the sounds and appearance of the blowhole at Mooloomba
7. northernmost, island
8. tribal, angry
9. a   10. d
11. accent   12. cord
13. stay; growl; said; told; was complaining
14. 'Wailing Rock' is where the old woman cried for help.

Answers

Maths

1. $x^2 = 1, 4, 9, 16, 25$
   $x^3 = 1, 8, 27, 64, 125$
2. 5.5
3. 0.85, 0.275, 0.45
4. $\frac{24}{1000}$, 0.024
5. positive
6. 9296
7. 14.655
8. $5\frac{13}{16}$
9. $18.81
10. $10:1$
11. all of them
12. $39 = 39$
13. $x = 6$
14. $7m$
15. 0.835 kg = 0.000835 t
16. 32.7 + 52.32 + 15.696
    = 100.716 cm
17. 1.92 m^2
18. 8741.816 cm^3
19.

20. (a)

    (b) right angle
21. $\frac{1}{20}$
22. 18.5

English

1. d   2. d
3. Make-up for TV is more natural.
4. the part hidden by the desk (the lower half)
5. I wish people were allowed to wear open-necked shirts and short sleeves.
6. b
7. Who advises you on how to dress?
8. There's tremendous competition on television nowadays.
9. d   10. b
11. vain
12. straight
13. Suggested answers: confidently, clearly
14. What happens after you've had your hair and make-up done?

Maths

1. $\frac{4}{3}$, 0.8, 76%, $\frac{4}{6}$, 0.099
2. $9 \times 10^4 + 7 \times 10^3 + 8 \times 10^2 + 6 \times 10^1 + 2 \times 10^0$
3. 7 hundred thousand
4. $\frac{5}{6}, \frac{16}{24}, \frac{4}{5}$
5. (a) rational
   (b) 3.1429
6. 2964
7. 7.003
8. $4\frac{1}{2}$ $4\left(\frac{5}{10}\right)$
9. 32
10. $4:7$
11. $6xy$
12. 7
13. $12 - 3a$
14. $w - 2$
15. 176 hours
16. 1.6 cm
17. 11 m
18. cube
19. surface, face, vertex, circle
20. 180°
21. $\frac{1}{4}$ (25%)
22. 4

English

1. a
2. b
3. Moorabbin
4. Bass Strait
5. helped
6. 'could not identify'; 'it is not an aircraft'
7. I especially liked reading this Australian UFO mystery.
8. A UFO sighting was reported at a quarter to seven yesterday.
9. c
10. b
11. converse
12. sewn, veil
13. because it was too dark
14. At the last Christmas concert, Jack played the part of Santa Claus in 'Angels Down Under'.

Maths

1. (a) 12   (b) 27
2. 24 780 084
3. (a) 37.2   (b) 37.25   (c) 37.248
4. (a) $\frac{9}{16}$ (b) $\frac{3}{5}$
5. 2
6. 149 160
7. 67
8. $2\frac{7}{12}$
9. 117
10. $2:1$
11. 5
12. 6
13. $-5p$
14. -24
15. 23 days
16. $28 \times 13 = 364$ m^2
17. 72.44 km
18. 1.76 L
19. supplementary
20. 360°
21. (a) $\frac{1}{3}$ (b) $\frac{1}{6}$
    (c) $\frac{1}{12}$ (d) $\frac{1}{4}$
22. 9 °C

English

1. c
2. b
3. d
4. rural
5. rural sector, family farms, small private businesses
6. to develop the economy
7. The greatest problem during the 1930s was unemployment.
8. Men collapsed from hunger and exhaustion.
9. a
10. c
11. sheer
12. staring
13. Suggested answers: running, dancing
14. Brisbane-born Sue Maylee has become the first Australian to win a British amateur title in darts.

Answers

Maths
1. 12.221
2. (c) −32
3. (c) 32.137
4. Yes
5. +1
6. 6289.2
7. 32.6455
8. $\frac{3}{5}$
9. $1350
10. 42:56
11. perimeter of a square
12. 35 cm²
13. Yes
14. $4x - y$
15. less than half an hour
16. 66.7 cm
17. 45 m
18. no difference
19.
20. *AXB, BXC, CXD, AXC, BXD, AXD*
21. $\frac{2}{9}$
22. (a) 15   (b) 15

English
1. a   2. b
3. with a passion
4. False
5. Suggested answers: to be part of a team; for entertainment
6. a
7. My favourite sports entertainment is hockey.
8. In November she visited her relatives.
9. b
10. b
11. reverse
12. presence
13. In this weather; about the only thing; in a hammock
14. The Diamonds won the Netball World Cup in 2023.

Maths
1. −304
2. no
3. 225, 252
4. (a) $\frac{15}{40} + \frac{16}{40} = \frac{31}{40}$
   (b) $\frac{10}{15} - \frac{3}{15} = \frac{7}{15}$
5. −6, −5, −1, +3, +7
6. 780   7. 4.981
8. 427 ÷ 11 and 616 ÷ 9
9. 126 km
10. 1:2
11. $b \times b \times c \times c \times c \times d \times d \times d \times d$
12. $x = 4a + 4b$
13. 5
14. 15 unit²
15. 5
16. ÷
17. 441 cm²
18. 520 mL
19. regular pentagon
20.   21.
22. 2

English
1. c   2. b
3. Sharing knowledge, skills and experience with another person to help them progress
4. Suggested answers: personal satisfaction, good for the economy
5. Concern about Australia's performance in Science, Technology, Engineering and Mathematics (STEM) subjects
6. Engineering, construction and business management
7. encouraged
8. Science, centres
9. d   10. a
11. court   12. patients
13. Suggested answers:
    (a) the clubhouse
    (b) the short tail
14. 'Congratulations! You got the job. You start on Monday. Good luck!' said the employer.

Maths
1. 2^8 (256) > 8^2 (64), 192
2. $(2 \times 2) \times (2 \times 2 \times 2) = 2 \times 2 \times 2 \times 2 \times 2 = 2^5$
3. 0.147
4. (a) $\frac{3}{8}$ (b) $\frac{4}{11}$
5. (a) 133.734
   (b) 0.56, 0.5, 0.056, 0.006, 0.005
6. $1110.50
7. 1.848 km
8. 48
9. 210 tonnes
10. 1:2:5
11. If $x = 12, y + 4$ and $z = 3$, then only (a) and (b) are correct.
12. $a(x + y)$ or $ax + ay$
13. $x + 1$
14.

x	0	1	2	3
y	6	4	2	0

15. 7800 g
16. 9.75 m
17. 720 mm²
18. 530 L
19. octagonal
20. *AXC, CXB, BXD, DXA*
21. $\frac{1}{13}$
22. 53

English
1. d
2. to access the news at any time of the day and on a variety of platforms
3. a pleasing sounding voice
4. to provide on-the-spot reports of international events
5. newsreaders
6. because the ABC gathers news from a variety of sources
7. overseas, international
8. missed
9. c
10. c
11. sheer
12. breeches
13. He, people, life
14. Uncle Georgio and Aunty Maria, who live in Greece, have sent me a postcard of the Acropolis.

Answers

Maths

1. 8
2. 48 734 182
3. (a) 432, 216, 108, 54, 27
   (b) 720, 360, 180, 90, 45
4. $\frac{16}{24} + \frac{12}{24} + \frac{6}{24} = \frac{34}{24}$ or $1\frac{10}{24}$ or $1\frac{5}{12}$
5. 12 floors
6. 1300   7. 8.47
8. 116 L   9. 67.77 m
10. $16, $24
11. $xa + xb + xc$
12. If $a = 2$ then $2a^2 = 8$ and $(2a)^2 = 16$; disprove
13. $y = x - 1$
14.

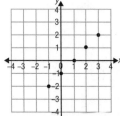

15. 6
16. $14p$ cm
17. 189 m^2
18. first container by 4.48 L
19. 8
20. 110°
21. 1 out of 3 chances $\left(\frac{1}{3}\right)$
22. (a) 6.9   (b) 6.94

English

1. c   2. c
3. Carlton   4. 19th century
5. Because his mother would keep him home on Fridays so they could go to the cinema.
6. Suggested answer: He saw a lot of the Victorian city and countryside.
7. He completed many paintings during the war years.
8. Nolan finished a series of Ned Kelly pictures.
9. c   10. b
11. sought
12. ally
13. Asked Grandma Jill.
14. Some NSW candidates belong to no political party at all. Are they called Independents?

Maths

1. (a) 1 000 000 + 400 000 + 60 000 + 30 + 7
   (b) $8 \times 10^6 + 7 \times 10^5 + 9 \times 10^2 + 3 \times 10^0$
2. $1 \times 10\,000\,000 + 2 \times 1\,000\,000 + 8 \times 100\,000 + 1 \times 10\,000 + 3 \times 1000 + 6 \times 100 + 4 \times 10 + 3 \times 1 + 5 \times 0.1$ $\left(\text{or } \frac{1}{10}\right)$
3. (a) 0.8̇
   (b) 0.3̇
   (c) 0.75
   (d) 0.08
   (e) 0.75
4. (a) 0.268
   (b) 1.358
   (c) 0.097
   (d) 0.009
5. −10
6. 0
7. (a) 750
   (b) 0.101
   (c) 219.214
8. $\frac{3}{16}$
9. 42 squares shaded
10. 2 : 3
11. 195
12. $\frac{3x}{4}$
13. $a = 7$
14. $b + 3b^2$
15. (a) 73 kg
    (b) 3 kg
    (c) 10 kg
    (d) 1 kg
16. 2.7 m
17. 600 mm^2
18. (a) L
    (b) mL or cm^3
    (c) cm^3
19.   pentagon
20. Suggested answer:

21. (a) True
    (b) False
    (c) True
22. 27 minutes

English

1. c
2. d
3. c
4. in a Cairo hotel
5. Superstition about the curse kept people away.
6. b
7. The tragedies were connected to the discovery of the tomb.
8. The sinister superstition is based on unconfirmed reports.
9. c
10. c
11. throne
12. bite
13. Parent/teacher to check
14. 'Did you see Aaron Hawkins at the Geelong Show last Thursday?' asked Shelley.

Answers

UNIT 16 page 46

Maths
1. 1 011 101 001
2. true
3. −372
4. (a) <   (b) >
5. −3
6. 98 730
7. 9 boxes
8. $\frac{3}{4}$
9. $4.50 (90 five-cent coins)
10. 8 cm
11. 9
12. $\frac{1000z}{y}$
13. $6y - 15$
14. −11
15. less
16. 6 cm
17. 84 cm²
18. 385 cm³
19. rays, vertex
20. 12, 18, 8
21. $\frac{1}{13}\left(\frac{8}{104}\right)$
22. 74.5

English
1. d
2. c
3. Uncle Jack's blue-tongue lizard.
4. a fritter
5. (His presents bring us) added gloom …
6. 1d, 2c, 3a, 4b
7. The tree was decorated with brilliant lights.
8. In the Netherlands, it's traditional to fill your shoes with hay and sugar before Christmas.
9. a
10. b
11. desert
12. hangar
13. except; and
14. 'My gift from Mrs Mason was made by her son Julius,' I commented.

UNIT 17 page 48

Maths
1. 21
2. thirty-seven and two hundred and sixty-four thousandths
3. (a) 5^7 (b) 11^3
4. (a) $\frac{13}{20}$ (b) $\frac{67}{200}$ (c) $\frac{27}{250}$
5. (a) 12.75   (b) 18.377
6. 22 372
7. $33.25
8. $4\left(\frac{4}{1}\right)$
9. $90
10. $48.75, $65.00
11. $(p + q) \div r$ or $\frac{p + q}{r}$
12. $x = -8$
13. (−2, −1)
14. $4 \times 2\,(2 + 6) = 64$
    $4 \times 2^2 + 24 \times 2 = 64$
    Correct
15. 10 kg
16. 750 m
17. 9600 cm²
18. (a) 2832 mL
    (b) 2.93 L
    (c) 0.1605
19. *ABFE, ABCD, EFGH, DCGH*
20. 40°, 70°, 100°
21. $\frac{1}{8}$
22. No

English
1. d   2. c
3. rupee
4. low because they are not well educated
5. true
6. migration from the country to the city
7. wet weather, decision, postpone
8. qualifications , offer
9. a
10. c
11. rung
12. varnish
13. command
14. 'All's well that ends well,' sighed Georgio as he closed his driving manual.

UNIT 18 page 50

Maths
1. 9, 21, 54, 14, 86
2. 56
3. $2^3 = 2 \times 2 \times 2$, $2^2 = 2 \times 2$
   $8 \times 4 = 32$
   $2^5 = 2 \times 2 \times 2 \times 2 \times 2 = 32$
   true
4. 0.6, 0.35, 0.035
5. 0.0007, 0.009, 0.089, 0.0897, 0.989
6. (a) false   (b) false
7. $2 \times 16 \times $60.50 = 1936
8. $2\frac{1}{8}$
9. $210
10. 4 : 1
11. $(x + 11) \div 4$ or $\frac{x + 11}{4}$
12. $2x + 1$
13. $x = -6$
14. 22
15. 840 times
16. 176 posts
17. 1200 mm²
18. 1.8225 kilometres
19. False
20. more than 12
21. (a) $\frac{5}{26}$ (b) $y, \frac{1}{26}$
22. 16 years, 170 cm

English
1. d   2. c
3. Chapter Four
4. False
5. Yes, page 15
6. because they all relate to safe swimming techniques
7. All the students enjoyed the windsurfing experience.
8. The swimmers were rescued from the mountainous waves near the rocky headland.
9. b   10. a
11. packed
12. lightning
13. I have good supplies of wool to complete the cargoes.
14. It's important for the rescuer to kneel beside the victim's side then perform CPR if need be.

Answers

ANSWERS: *Excel* Basic Skills English and Mathematics Year 7

UNIT 19 page 52

Maths

1. multiply by 1000
2. 1 025 000 000
3. (a) 11.7 (b) 11.719
4. $\frac{5}{6}, \frac{7}{9}, \frac{1}{2}, \frac{1}{3}, \frac{1}{9}$
5. 0.75
6. 4752
7. $57.80
8. $1\frac{13}{16}$
9. $889.92
10. 4 cm
11. (d) $x \times y \times z$
12. 22
13. 6
14. a diamond/rhombus
15. 20%
16. 30 cm
17. 8 cm
18. 10 cm
19. triangular prism
20. True
21. $\frac{1}{2}$
22. 51, 43, 38, 32, 27, 24, ㉒ 19, 17, 16, 16, 15, 12

English

1. c
2. c
3. ☆☆☆☆☆ (Excellent, Fabuloso!)
4. Nicki
5. visual effects produced by technological means to make a movie more spectacular
6. 1d, 2b, 3a, 4c
7. Peter boasted that he was capable of doing much better.
8. They were especially sorry they missed the opening moments of the film.
9. d
10. b
11. slight
12. There
13. (a) dearer (b) younger
14. Mrs BC Whiteman gave Mr TC Smithers an award for best playwright.

UNIT 20 page 54

Maths

1. 9, 25, 49
2. 8 018 030 709
3. 0.19, 0.25, $\frac{6}{20}$, 32%, $\frac{1}{3}$
4. (a) $\frac{13}{5}$ (b) $\frac{67}{12}$ (c) $\frac{67}{10}$
5. a
6. 16.2375 t
7. 9 588.53
8. $8\frac{1}{30}$
9. $57 600
10. (a) 1:30 (b) 5:1
11. 2
12. $2ab$
13. (−3, −2)
14. True
15. (a) 04:27 (b) 18:21
16. 1.210 048
17. 84 cm^2
18. (a) 0.75 L (b) 750 mL
19. 6,8
20. (a) *BXC, CXD, DXE, BXD, CXE, BXE*
    (b) *BXC* = 69° *CXD* = 47°
    DXE = 133° *BXD* = 116°
    CXE = 180° *BXE* = 249°
21. 50% (1 in 2)
22. 8

English

1. a
2. b
3. insoluble
4. kJ
5. Suggested answer: so people can make an informed choice about what they're eating
6. False
7. She applied for the position of Principal at our school.
8. Is the data correctly listed in the directory?
9. d
10. c
11. lapse
12. greater
13. Parent/teacher to check
14. 'We didn't catch a single fish,' John complained as he took off his muddy, black gumboots.

UNIT 21 page 56

Maths

1. 2, 6, 12, 20, 30
2. 4 027 706 914
3. (a) positive (b) negative (c) false
4. 25 minutes
5. 4 intervals
6. 451 991
7. (a) 5.4̇5̇ (b) 6.3̇6̇
8. $4\frac{17}{36}$
9. 25%
10. 5:8
11. $\frac{160z}{y}$
12. 36
13. $a = 3$
14. (−3, 2)
15. Monday
16. 21.6 cm, or 0.216 m
17. 600 cm^2
18. 4050 cm^3
19. cylinder
20. (a) 142° (b) 142° (c) 142°
21. 6
22. 2

English

1. b
2. c
3. the member of government for Smithville
4. because it's separated by a median strip and guard rail
5. Suggested answers: Because it is rough; it forces people to detour onto the roadway.
6. d
7. Thomas keeps complaining about his assignments and homework.
8. Many of the letters received by the council were addressed to the local Member.
9. d
10. c
11. captives
12. corpse
13. Broken
14. Did you collect the babies' blankets and put them in their cots?

A8

Answers

UNIT 22 page 58

Maths

1. 13 787 600, 13 787 750, 13 787 900
2. 33, 977
3. 24
4. $\frac{2}{5}, \frac{4}{5}, \frac{1}{200}, \frac{1}{80}$
5. +3
6. $299.10; $100.90
7. $2.55
8. $\frac{5}{8}$
9. $3256
10. 460
11. $6(7 + 7^2 - 5) = 306$
12. $\frac{100m}{x}$
13. $-4 - 7a$
14. $x = 16$
15. $1.11
16. 55.8 km
17. 96 cm²
18. 32 768 L (32.768 m³)
19. pentagon
20. 111°
21. $\frac{1}{13}$
22. 13

English

1. d
2. c
3. a recent council meeting
4. to not swim at the beach until the nets have been repaired
5. apprehension, danger
6. Yes; damage to the nets creates a risk to beachgoers. The damage wasn't serious.
7. The council was embarrassed about the news article.
8. Make up your own opinion about the headline and the story.
9. b
10. b
11. checked
12. Lay
13. Parent/teacher to check
14. 'Why wasn't action taken any sooner?' demanded Mr Wilson.

UNIT 23 page 60

Maths

1. False
2. −2
3. 30.1447
4. $1\frac{39}{56}$
5. 192 °C
6. 182
7. $1.38
8. $1\frac{1}{6}$
9. $472.83
10. $320
11. $24x^2y^2$
12. $-8x^2 - 24$
13.

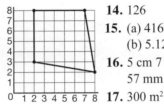

14. 126
15. (a) 4163 kg
    (b) 5.127 kg
16. 5 cm 7 mm, 57 mm
17. 300 m²
18. cube
19. circle
20. 50°
21. 26 runs
22. 35

English

1. a
2. c
3. Household, industrial
4. paper/cardboard
5. Suggested answer: because it is easiest to sort/recycle
6. Suggested answer: we could be recycling a lot more
7. Most plastic packaging is disposed of as garbage.
8. Food scraps and garden waste can be used as compost.
9. a
10. b
11. council
12. draught
13. The waste was removed by several of the workers.
14. Use bags, baskets and boxes to carry shopping purchases. Avoid collecting plastic bags.

TEST 3 page 62

Maths

1. (a) 3 107 000 343
   (b) one hundred and one point one zero one
2. 12, 68, 220, 516, 1004
3. 2^4
4. 47% = 0.47; 32% = 0.32; 50% = 0.5; 1% = $\frac{1}{100}$; 270% = $\frac{27}{10}$
5. $\frac{16}{3} = 5\frac{1}{3}, \frac{12}{3} = 4; \frac{15}{3} = 5, \frac{9}{3} = 3, \frac{6}{3} = 2$
6. 30 176   7. 84 boxes
8. $4\frac{5}{12}$
9. $1448.40
10. A:B   1250:1600   25:32
11. $\frac{x^2y^2}{3}$
12. correct
13. 10
14. [graph]
15. 17 013 kg
16. 3.75 km
17. 4050 cm²
18. 35 glasses
19. depth
20. 30°
21. $\frac{1}{4}$
22. (a) 2   (b) 3   (c) 2

English

1. d   2. c   3. d
4. Ash Wednesday bushfires
5. provided information on the extent of the fires, damage, safety of friends and relatives, and where it was safe
6. c
7. The work of radio journalists provides a valuable community service.
8. The reporter said there was absolutely nothing that could be done to prevent his home from being destroyed.
9. c
10. c
11. source
12. story
13. good
14. 'Why,' asked the girl, 'did you not even bother to have the equipment repaired?'

ANSWERS: *Excel* Basic Skills English and Mathematics Year /

Answers

UNIT 24 page 66

Maths

1. (a) >   (b) =
2. $1 \times 10^1 + 6 \times 10^0 + \dfrac{5}{10^1} + \dfrac{7}{10^3} + \dfrac{9}{10^4}$
3. (a) 16.9   (b) 16.874   (c) 20
4. one-third, $\dfrac{4}{9}$, $\dfrac{5}{11}$, $0.\dot{6}$
5. 19.9692
6. 13 967
7. 4.667
8. 6
9. 80%
10. $A = \$744.96$ $B = \$588.72$
11. $l \times l \times l \times l$
12.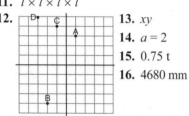
13. xy
14. $a = 2$
15. 0.75 t
16. 4680 mm
17. 38 cm
18. 50 times
19. $1 : 3$
20. (a) 67°   (b) 113°   (c) 69°
21. $\dfrac{7}{12}$
22. 67

English

1. d   2. c
3. A plot of land.
4. The (snarling) squatter.
5. Suggested answers: dejected, sad, bored
6. because he was cheerful and brave
7. The extract is part of a ballad which was originally a story set to music.
8. He looked slightly built alongside many of his opponents.
9. c
10. d
11. affect
12. stationary
13. (I) read the poem which (you) suggested.
14. He said that he had been there before.

UNIT 25 page 68

Maths

1. 4 097 406
2. 24.3752
3. 6 000 370 089
4. (a) $5\dfrac{2}{3}$ (b) $3\dfrac{2}{9}$
5. =
6. 345
7. 173 004.25
8. $12\dfrac{1}{4}$
9. $54.72
10. 36 cm
11. $(x - 4y)$
12. $-8 + 12w$
13. 18
14. 5 units
15. 26 g (0.026 kg)
16. 670 m
17. $a(x + y)$
18. 4.38 L or 4380 mL
19. Parent/teacher to check; 143°
20. 60°
21. HH, HT, TH, TT
22. 15

English

1. d   2. d   3. 3
4. cracked wheat
5. none
6. (1) covering burghul with cold water (2) allowing burghul to soak for half an hour
(3) spreading burghul out to dry
(4) combining olive oil and lemon juice
7. In the debating team, I represented the affirmative side.
8. Have you included quotation marks in the factual text?
9. d
10. b
11. cited
12. mete
13. adverb
14. 'What a lovely morning it is!' Val exclaimed. 'Let's go for a walk through the Botanical Gardens.'

UNIT 26 page 70

Maths

1. 48
2. (a) 1, 4, 9, 16, 25
   (b) 1, 8, 27, 64, 125
3. (a) 60   (b) 56
4. $\dfrac{5}{12}, \dfrac{1}{2}, \dfrac{2}{3}, \dfrac{3}{4}, \dfrac{5}{6}$
5. true   6. 479 048
7. $109.50   8. $\dfrac{13}{21}$
9. 10%
10. Container A 375 mL
    Container B 625 mL
    Total 1000 mL
11. $-6a$
12. $\dfrac{n - x}{2}$ 13.
14. 3
15. 48 kg
16. 16 027 m
17. 25 m
18. 1 L water = 1 kg = 1000 cm³
19. *BUTA, BUVD, BACD*
20. (a) $\angle c$ (b) supplementary
    (c) 360°
21. $\dfrac{5}{8}$ 22.

Score	Frequency
7	4
8	7
9	3
10	5

English

1. c   2. c
3. having long experience in the field
4. a reusable space vehicle
5. to gather support for further scientific work in space
6. because it resparked interest in the space program
7. He has an appointment with his solicitor at a quarter to eleven.
8. The migratory habits of some birds are really most remarkable.
9. b   10. d
11. trussed
12. prise
13. quickly
14. Oddly, it took him until 1982, when he was twenty-four, to win the Australian Singles title for the first time.

Answers

UNIT 27 page 72

Maths

1. $-224 > -240$
2. 9990
3. -143
4. (a) 48   (b) 85.5
5. ground floor
6. 38 625
7. 111.684
8. 280 children
9. 16
10. $x : z : y$
11. $\dfrac{x + y}{w - z}$
12. 301
13. $\dfrac{a + b + c}{3}$
14. (4, 3)
15. 29
16. 12 pieces (13th piece is not 80 cm so it is not counted)
17. 0.225 m²
18. 60×250 mL, 150×500 mL
19. hexagonal pyramid
20. 45°
21. $\dfrac{1}{2}$
22. 7

English

1. b
2. d
3. an article or column presenting opinions
4. S Pullard
5. They are fed-up/complaining.
6. opinion
7. Connective tissues hold the various structures of the body together.
8. Repetitive pressure on the bones may lead to stress fractures.
9. d
10. b
11. martial
12. source
13. Suggested answers: because, when she heard
14. These crops are found in the Grantham district: wheat, oats, barley and potatoes.

UNIT 28 page 74

Maths

1. $<$
2. (a) 10.1   (b) 10.09   (c) 10.087
3. 7, 25, 61, 95, 385
4. (a) $\dfrac{52}{7}$ (b) $\dfrac{83}{12}$
5. true
6. 182 250
7. 0.671 (0.999 − 0.328)
8. 72
9. $11 511.50
10. $240, $180
11. $bc - (y - z)$
12. 27
13. 4
14. True
15. 168
16. 20.836 m (or 2083.6 cm; 20 836 mm)
17. $1280
18. 800 mL
19.

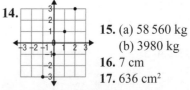

20. *ABD* and *CBG*
21. $\dfrac{7}{24}$
22. 11.4

English

1. a   2. b
3. a full-length, jointed, three-dimensional puppet worked by strings and wires
4. to create lifelike movement
5. 'Puppet' is a general term to describe any manipulated figure; 'marionette' is a puppet manipulated by strings and wires.
6. Yes, the puppet's movements could be made more precise.
7. Shadow puppets are usually flat, cut-out figures.
8. The Muppets are a combination of hand and rod puppets.
9. d   10. d
11. from
12. off
13. the toy soldier
14. Attach the following pieces: eyes, mouth, hair, moustache and ears.

UNIT 29 page 76

Maths

1. 3 000 359 648
2. $\dfrac{5}{8}$, 63%, 0.701, 4.5
3. 3.992, 3.99   4. $0.2\dot{7}$
5. -9 6. 768
7. 9.844   8. $162.50
9. $52.00   10. 1 : 16
11. If $x = 12$, $y = 3$ and $z = 2$ then $2 \neq 8$
12. $\dfrac{1\,000\,000\,yn}{m}$
13.

x	-1	0	1	2
y	-3	-1	1	3

14.
15. (a) 58 560 kg
    (b) 3980 kg
16. 7 cm
17. 636 cm²
18. cube 262 144 cm³
    prism 230 048 cm³
    cube is larger
19. kite
20. (a) 1080°   (b) 45°
21. $1.01, -\dfrac{1}{2}$ 22. 17

English

1. Suggested answer: Nan is always using her hands to do tasks.
2. c
3. Suggested answers: Nan teaches her, comforts her, listens to her.
4. a comfortable chair or a sunny spot in the garden
5. She wipes her granddaughter's tears and gives her hugs.
6. c
7. He managed to produce a supreme effort for the last lap of the race.
8. Which golfing achievement of yours do you consider to be the most memorable?
9. d   10. b
11. draft   12. manner
13. Parent/teacher to check
14. Suggested answer: Many of them said, 'We have finished the work early.'

Answers

Maths

1. 2 070 608 506
2. −8, −5, 0, 40, 72
3. 0.0058, 0.0085, 0.85, 0.855, 0.8851
4. (a) $1\frac{3}{8}$ (b) $\frac{9}{28}$
5. [number line marked with points at −5, −3, 0, 4]
   −6 −5   −3   0   4   6
6. 367 655
7. 8744.48
8. $2\frac{3}{8}$
9. 90%
10. 374
11. $5t$ km
12. $3x$ m^2
13. −2
14. $a = 3\frac{1}{2}$
15. 50 g
16. $20y$ cm
17. 325 000 cm^2 (32.5 m^2)
18. 3762 cm^3
19. (a) 0   (b) 5
    (c) 4   (d) apex
20. $\angle a = 80°$; $\angle b = 40°$; $\angle c = 60°$
21. $\frac{4}{8}$ or $\frac{1}{2}$
22. 6

English

1. c
2. b
3. exhilarating
4. sensational styling, classic looks
5. exhilarating performance on track or road
6. cutting edge
7. Which safety features are emphasised in the motorbike advertisement?
8. The motorbike has an exceptional braking system.
9. d
10. b
11. Bridle
12. their
13. Suggested answer: The workers were unhappy about collecting the machine.
14. Was the engine for the Macro 1100 developed by Allen and Co. in Melbourne?

Maths

1. $y^2 = 1, 4, 9, 16, 25$
   $y^3 = 1, 8, 27, 64, 125$
2. −2
3. 18. Suggested answer:

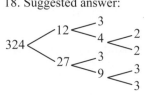

4. (a) 0.625   (b) $62\frac{1}{2}$%   (c) 5 : 8
5. (a) −4, −3, −2
   (b) +4, +5, +6
   (c) −11, −10, −9
   (d) 0, +1, +2
6. 35
7. 20.13
8. $721.50
9. 27% of $150
10. 2 : 7 : 12
11. $9 + 2.5 − 6 = 5.5$
    $\frac{3+5}{2} = 4$
    Incorrect
12. $2a − 7$
13. $−2a − ab$
14. $p = 7$
15. 9.783 t or 9783 kg
16. 10.9 m
17. 324 m^2
18. 27 extra cups
19. B
20. 160°
21. 5
22. 3.8

English

1. d
2. c
3. b
4. the unexplained girl watching them
5. Because she was glad to see her father.
6. Because it was a big change in their lives; they're taking note of their new surroundings.
7. The jetty was sheltered from the wind and reasonably calm.
8. The children collapsed on the grassy patch.
9. d
10. c
11. slight
12. sheer
13. Suggested answer: The child was happy to mend the ncts.
14. She said that we'd go up to the old house first.

Measurement and Space

15. Round off to the nearest kilogram.

(a) 72.985 kg _____

(b) 3.2 kg _____

(c) 9.5 kg _____

(d) 0.555 kg _____

16. Which measurement shows a suitable height for a delivery truck? _____

17 m   2.7 m   3 km   14 cm   5982 mm

17. Measure the triangle and then find the area.
Answer in mm².

_____

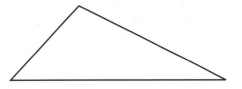

18. Find the missing units of measurement.

(a) 1000 _____ = 1 kilolitre   (b) 1000 _____ = 1 L   (c) 1 000 000 _____ = 1 m³

19. This is a regular pentagon. Draw in all of the diagonals.
What is the plane shape formed at the very centre? _____

20. Show the angle 60°
on the clock face.

Statistics and Probability

21. The following coloured discs were placed in a box: 3 red, 6 green, 4 white and 3 black.
Are the following statements true or false?

(a) Red and black have an equal chance of being drawn. _____

(b) White has 4 chances in 17 of being selected. _____

(c) You would have twice the chance of selecting a green than a black. _____

22. The amount of time, in minutes, spent by six students on homework one night is shown in
the table.

Children	John	Kate	Beau	Scott	Spiro	Lee
Time spent	35	5	55	15	20	30

What is the mean, to the nearest minute? _____

The Curse of Tutankhamun

What was the strange power of the inscription found in the tomb of an Egyptian boy king? Was it a curse, made thousands of years ago, which was responsible for the extraordinary events which followed the discovery of the tomb of Tutankhamun?

It was a hot November day, 1922 in the Valley of the Kings in Egypt. After years of searching, the archaeologist, Howard Carter, had finally found what he believed to be the resting place of the boy-king, Tutankhamun, who had been buried about the year 1000 BC—three thousand years ago.

In great excitement he sent a telegram to his sponsor, Lord Carnarvon in England, so that he could be there when they opened the tomb. Lord Carnarvon arrived soon after, and on February 16 1923, they broke through the door to find one of the most amazing archaeological discoveries of all time.

There were four rooms containing caskets, a gold throne inlaid with precious stones, gems, furniture, clothing and weapons. In the burial chamber itself, flanked by two black statues, were four gold shrines, one inside the other, and a nest of three coffins. The inner one, of solid gold, held the mummified body of Tutankhamun, wrapped in a jewel-studded shroud. Over his face was a gold mask inlaid with precious stones.

Howard Carter and Lord Carnarvon were stunned by the splendour of their find, relics which are among the richest the world has ever seen. They also found an inscription above the tomb, which they were able to translate. It read: 'Death will come to those who disturb the sleep of the pharaohs.'

What was to follow was a chain of strange deaths and tragedies affecting more than a dozen people who had been connected somehow by the discovery of the tomb. Victims, perhaps of the pharaoh's curse?

This sinister superstition is based on unconfirmed reports of disturbing happenings that began on the very day Howard Carter and Lord Carnarvon and their work party entered the tomb. As the last man climbed back into the sunshine, a sandstorm is said to have sprung up and swirled over the mouth of the cave, and as it died away, a hawk, the royal emblem of ancient Egypt, was seen soaring over the tomb. The bird is the spirit of the dead pharaoh, who has left his curse on those who had tampered with his tomb, said some in fear.

Five months later, Lord Carnarvon, aged fifty-seven, was bitten by a mosquito on the left cheek. The bite became infected and led to blood poisoning. As Lord Carnarvon died in a Cairo hotel, the entire lights of the city suddenly went out. At the same time, at Lord Carnarvon's home in Hampshire, England, his dog howled for several minutes, then fell dead. Strangest of all, doctors who later examined Tutankhamun's mummified body, reported finding a mark on his left cheek exactly corresponding to the place of Lord Carnarvon's mosquito bite.

In the following years, the curse was blamed for the deaths of several others who had visited the tomb. An Egyptian prince, Ali Farmy Bey, who claimed to be descended from the pharaohs, was murdered, and his brother killed himself. An American railway tycoon, George Jay Gould, died of pneumonia after catching a cold in the tomb. The Hon. Richard Bethell, who helped Howard Carter catalogue the treasures, was said to have committed suicide for no apparent reason, and a few months later, his father hurled himself to his death from the window of his London flat. An alabaster vase from the tomb was in his bedroom.

More than a dozen people who had been concerned in one way or another with the discovery of the tomb died unnatural deaths.

From *Strange Mysteries* by Rachael Collinson

Reading and Comprehension

1. Who was the man who sponsored Howard Carter?
   (a) Richard Bethell
   (b) George Gould
   (c) Lord Carnarvon
   (d) Ali Farmy Bey

2. The burial chamber was flanked by
   (a) four gold shrines.
   (b) inlaid gold masks.
   (c) precious gems and furniture.
   (d) two black statues.

3. The disturbing happenings began
   (a) before Lord Carnarvon arrived from England.
   (b) when the sponsor returned home.
   (c) the day the tomb was opened.
   (d) a few months after the tomb opening.

4. Where did Lord Carnarvon die?

   _____

5. What explanation could be given as to how the ancient tomb had remained intact for so long?

   _____

   _____

   _____

6. What is the author's intention?
   (a) to tell about the treasures in the tomb
   (b) to suggest that the deaths may have had something to do with the curse
   (c) to explain how several people associated with the tomb died
   (d) to praise the work of Howard Carter and his sponsor

Spelling and Vocabulary

Rewrite the misspelt words.

7. The trajedies were connected to the discovry of the tomb.

   _____

8. This sinistir superstition is based on uncomfirmed reports.

   _____

Circle the word that has the nearest meaning to the underlined word.

9. To many people the events in the story had a supernatural quality.
   (a) unparalleled
   (b) sympathetic
   (c) mystic
   (d) tolerant

10. The American railway tycoon died of pneumonia.
    (a) explorer
    (b) archaeologist
    (c) magnate
    (d) sponsor

Circle the correct word in brackets.

11. The golden (thrown / throne) was in the corner of the tomb.

12. The (bight / bite) from the small creature became infected.

Grammar and Punctuation

13. Add a clause containing an adverb indicating time to this simple sentence.

    Yesterday she saw the mask;

    _____

    _____

    _____

14. Punctuate and capitalise this sentence.

    did you see aaron hawkins at the geelong show last thursday asked shelley

    _____

    _____

    _____

Number and Algebra

1. Write one billion, eleven million, one hundred and one thousand and one hundred hundredths in digit form. _____

2. Ivan made a factor tree for a particular number and found that it has exactly four identical factors less than 100. It was a square number. ☐ True ☐ False

3. What is the value of $\frac{1}{8}$ of –2976? _____

4. Which sign < or > will complete these?

    (a) $\frac{4}{5}$ _____ $\frac{5}{6}$ (b) $\frac{5}{12}$ _____ $\frac{3}{8}$

5. Study this number line.

    ```
    ←─┬──┬──┬──┬──┬──┬──┬──┬──┬──┬──┬──┬──┬──→
     –6 –5 –4 –3 –2 –1  0 +1 +2 +3 +4 +5 +6
    ```

    4 is seven intervals right of A.
    Find A. _____

6. $(9350 – 3865) \times 18 =$ _____

7. The contents of 24 boxes each containing 132 apples were repacked into boxes each holding 96 apples. How many additional boxes were needed? _____

8. $\frac{2}{3}$ divided by $\frac{8}{9} =$ _____

9. Decrease $150 by 97% and express the result in five-cent coins. _____

10. The lengths of two chains are in the ratio of 2 : 5. If the longer chain is 20 cm, what is the length of the shorter chain? _____

11. Solve $45 – n = \frac{108}{3}$. _____

12. Express in algebraic form. How many packets of coffee each holding y grams can be filled with z kilograms of coffee? _____

13. Expand $3(2y – 5)$. _____

14. If $p = –4$ and $q = 3$, what is the value of $2p – q$? _____

Measurement and Space

15. Sixteen bales of wool averaging 142 kg were loaded onto an 8.5-tonne truck. Was the total mass more or less than 13 tonnes? _____

16. An equilateral triangle has a side length of 8 cm. The triangle and a square have the same perimeter. What is the length of each side of the square? _____

17. The area of a rhombus is found by halving the product of the diagonals. Find the area if the diagonals are 12 cm and 14 cm.

    _____

18. Increase each given dimension by 2 cm, then find the volume.

    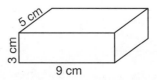

    _____

19. Fill in the missing words.

    An angle is formed from two r_____

    that have a common endpoint called the

    v_____.

20. How many vertices, edges and faces (including bases) has a hexagonal prism? _____

Statistics and Probability

21. When two full packs of cards are used, what are the chances of drawing an ace?

    _____

22. A golf player records his scores over 4 rounds of a tournament.

79	71	76	72

    What was the mean score? _____

Christmas visitor

Uncle Jack belongs outback
So when he comes to visit,
He brings along his kangaroo
And Bert, his blue-tongue lizard.

He decorates the Christmas tree
With lots of slimy critters
And then he turns the lights up high
And makes snakeburger fritters.

Jack also brings his cattle dog—
It bites off posties' limbs.
On Christmas Eve it stays awake,
Howling sacred hymns.

Uncle carves the turkey up:
Half for him and half for Pup,
And when it's time to have dessert,
He swipes my share to give to Bert!

His kangaroo sits at the table,
On the lap of Auntie Mabel.
It chews away on Christmas cake
And Auntie's finger (by mistake).

After lunch, Jack tells us that
He'll show us how to shear the cat.
His presents bring us added gloom;
A gift-wrapped spider's in my room.

From *That Smell is My Brother!* by Bill Condon

Reading and Comprehension

1. Why does Uncle Jack treat his animals so well?
(a) He has few friends.
(b) He is lonely in the outback.
(c) Humans and animals can develop special bonds in the outback.
(d) all of the above

2. Which word in the poem means 'hallowed'?
(a) gloom   (b) howling
(c) sacred   (d) swipes

3. Who is Bert?

_____

4. What name is given to a small food item made of batter which is often fried?

_____

5. Which phrase indicates the writer's disappointment with Jack's gift-giving practices?

_____

6. Number these events in order from 1 to 4.
(a) eats the Xmas cake   _____
(b) shear the feline   _____
(c) steals half my dessert   _____
(d) brings his kangaroo   _____

Spelling and Vocabulary

Rewrite the misspelt words.

7. The tree was decorited with brillant lights.

_____

8. In the Netherlands, it's traditonal to fil your shoes with hey and sugar befor Christmas.

_____

Circle the word that has the nearest meaning to the underlined word.

9. <u>Substitute</u> the raisins for the sultanas.
(a) replace   (b) subside   (c) master   (d) alternate

10. He had a <u>sullen</u> face on Christmas morning.
(a) amiable   (b) gloomy   (c) sultry   (d) studious

Circle the correct word in brackets.

11. Many of the soldiers decided to (desert / dessert) their comrades.

12. At the end of every flight the space shuttle is stored in its (hanger / hangar).

Grammar and Punctuation

13. Underline the conjunctions.

All the girls except Susannah played cooperatively and happily.

14. Punctuate and capitalise this sentence.

my gift from mrs mason was made by her son julius i commented

_____

_____

Mathematics

Number and Algebra

1. Find the highest common factor (HCF) of 42 and 63. _____

2. Write in words 37.264.

   _____

3. Complete the following equations.
   (a) $5^3 \times 5^4 = 5^\square$ _____
   (b) $11^5 \div 11^\square = 11^2$ _____

4. Express as simplified fractions.
   (a) 0.65 _____ (b) 0.335 _____
   (c) 0.108 _____

5. Round off 12.749 to
   the nearest hundredth. _____
   Round off 18.3768 to
   the nearest thousandth. _____

6. Use your calculator to find the product of 329 by 68 and check your result by division. _____

7. Add 0.25 of $12.60 to the difference between $60 and $29.90. _____

8. Divide $1\frac{1}{5}$ by $\frac{3}{10}$. _____

9. The prices of all phones in a shop are reduced by 5%. What is the discount on a phone priced at $1800? _____

10. Share $113.75 in the ratio 3:4. _____

11. Create an algebraic expression that means 'The sum of p and q divided by r'.

    _____

12. Solve $\frac{x}{4} = -2$. _____

13. The triangle PQR is reflected about the y-axis.

    What are the coordinates of the image of point R?

    _____

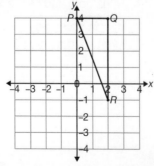

14. Verify that the equation $4\,l(l+6) = 4\,l^2 + 24\,l$ is indeed correct by substituting 2 for l.
    ☐ Correct ☐ Incorrect

Measurement and Space

15. Baby Jack weighs 7 kg. His weight is increasing by 500 g each month. In 6 months what will he weigh? _____

16. 0.75 of 1 km = _____ m

17. What area would the pages of a 60-page book cover if each page was 16 cm by 10 cm wide?
    Count 1 side of the page only. _____

18. Complete.
    (a) 3.1 L – 268 mL = _____ mL
    (b) 14.65 L ÷ 5 = _____ L
    (c) 3210 cm³ × 50 = _____ m³

19. Name 4 surfaces perpendicular to surface $ADHE$. _____

    _____

    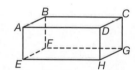

20. An isosceles triangle has an angle measuring 40°. From this list, circle other possible angles in the triangle.
    25°   40°   70°   100°

Statistics and Probability

21. The chance of landing on yellow or green is the same. The probability of red is twice the chance of blue. The probability of yellow or green equals the chance of blue.

    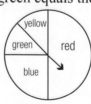

    What is the probability of spinning green?

    _____

22. A divided bar graph was drawn to represent the money saved by 3 people; a total of $80. Tran saved $40, Eoin $10 and Jessica $30. Does the graph represent the savings correctly?

    _____

An Indian Story

Madana and Madhu live in India. It is a country that has emerged from a long period of hibernation. What has changed?

Madana and Madhu are farmers but they want a better life for themselves. In the villages there are not many schools and many Indians want a full education. Many farmers want to earn more money so they can give their children a better life.

This 'internal migration' to city areas like New Delhi (capital) has seen an explosive boom. India has a population of about 1.7 billion. In New Delhi about 10 000 people squeeze into a space of about one square kilometre.

But a new life in the city has proven difficult for Madana and Madhu. City resources have been stressed due to this trend. It is a double-edged sword. The pay is minimal because they don't have a good education. They need to earn thousands of rupees per month to survive but they can't find a suitable job. More people means competition is an issue.

In the same breath, it is lonely for them too because they don't know anyone. How can they save money to bring their loved ones to the city?

The government has made moves to slow the country's population growth. It is predicted that if plans aren't enacted India may become the first country on Earth to reach the two billion mark!

Madana and Madhu want to start a family but they have been told to postpone this. Years ago, an Indian woman had six children.

Madana and Madhu are survivors because they have their youth, each other and hope for the future.

Reading and Comprehension

1. The two people mentioned in this story are
    (a) brother and sister.   (b) first cousins.
    (c) New Delhians.   (d) husband and wife.

2. Madana and Madhu wanted
    (a) to visit their loved ones in the city.
    (b) a change of scenery.
    (c) a better quality life for themselves.
    (d) to invest in some city resources.

3. What is the Indian currency unit mentioned?

_____

4. Would the income of Madana and Madhu in New Delhi be high or low? Explain your response.

_____

_____

5. Madana and Madhu have put off having a family. True or false? _____

6. What is meant by 'internal migration'?

_____

_____

Spelling and Vocabulary

Rewrite the misspelt words.

7. Because of the wet weathor the decison was made to postpoan sports day.

_____

8. What qualificatons and skills can you offerr ?

_____

Circle the word that has the nearest meaning to the underlined word.

9. A multinational corporation is sometimes made up of a <u>conglomeration</u> of other smaller ones.
    (a) collection (b) element (c) unit (d) recipe

10. The man bears a striking <u>resemblance</u> to a famous film star.
    (a) distinction   (b) difference
    (c) similarity   (d) appearance

Circle the correct word in brackets.

11. The bell was (wrung / rung) at three o'clock.

12. This is the (vanish / varnish) Jani used on the antique cabinet.

Grammar and Punctuation

13. Is this sentence a statement, question, command or exclamation?
    Pass the salt please, sir.

_____

14. Punctuate and capitalise this sentence.
    alls well that ends well sighed georgio as he closed his driving manual

_____

_____

Number and Algebra

1. Complete:

$x =$	2	4	7	3	9
$x^2 + 5 =$					

2. The lowest common multiple (LCM) of 2, 7 and 8 is _____.

3. $2^3 \times 2^2 = 2^5$
   Prove this by finding the value of each exponent and performing the calculation. Show your work.
   The statement is ☐ True   ☐ False.

4. Express the following as decimal fractions.
   $\frac{3}{5}$ _____ $\frac{7}{20}$ _____ $\frac{7}{200}$ _____

5. Arrange in ascending order of magnitude.
   0.089, 0.009, 0.989, 0.0007, 0.0897

   _____

6. Are these equations true or false?
   (a) $144 \div 8 + 16 = 121 \div 11 - (5 - 3)$ _____
   (b) $180 - 9 \times 5 \times 4 = 9 \times 0 + 45 \times 3$ _____

7. Banners are placed along both sides of an avenue. The length of the avenue is 150 metres. If banners are placed at 10-metre intervals and the cost of each banner and its installation is $60.50, what is the total cost of the decoration? _____

8. From three and three-quarters, subtract one and five-eighths. The answer is _____.

9. An item of furniture was sold at auction for $240. The auctioneer was paid $12\frac{1}{2}\%$ commission. What did the seller receive for the sale? _____

10. Simplify the ratio 2 metres : 50 centimetres.

    _____

11. If the perimeter of a square is $x + 11$, then the length of one side is _____.

12. How many apples must be added to x apples to make y apples? _____

13. What is the solution to
    $x + 4 = -2$? _____

14. If $P = 2l + 2b$, find P when $l = 8$ and $b = 3$.

    _____

Measurement and Space

15. A timing light flashes every 15 seconds. How many times will it flash in 3.5 hours? _____

16. Two posts are 1.75 km apart on the roadside of a paddock. Other posts are set up between them at intervals of 10 metres. How many posts are used altogether? _____

17. A triangular price tag has a base of 60 mm and a perpendicular height of 40 mm. What is the area? _____

18. How many kilolitres would there be in 45 vats each containing 40.5 litres? _____

19. A square is the same as a rhombus is the same as a quadrilateral. True or false? _____

20. How many triangles can be seen in this figure?
    less than 8
    between 8 and 12
    more than 12

Statistics and Probability

21. Suzi has a bag containing 26 cards. Each card has a different letter of the alphabet on it.
    (a) What is the chance of drawing out a vowel? _____
    (b) Which letter is a consonant but also can be termed as a vowel? _____
        What is the chance of drawing it? _____

22. James completed this table about the age and height of people in his family. What is the median age and median height?

Person	Age	Height (cm)
Dad	36	176
Brother	15	170
Sister	13	161
Sister	16	168
Mum	35	171

Table of contents

Reading and Comprehension

1. The table of contents does not convey

   (a) the pages topics appear on.

   (b) the purpose of the book.

   (c) the topics you can read about in the book.

   (d) information about the authors and illustrators.

2. How many pages does the chapter on rescue techniques have?

   (a) 88 pages   (b) 4 pages

   (c) 28 pages   (d) 94 pages

3. In which chapter would you be able to find how to cope with life-threatening situations?

4. True or false? Sidestroke and breaststroke techniques are not topics listed in this book.

5. Is there a section which details the purpose of the book? If so, on what page does it start?

6. Why are the topics in Chapter 2 grouped together?

Spelling and Vocabulary

Rewrite the misspelt words.

7. All the studants enjoyed the windsurfing experence.

8. The swimmers were rescued from the mountainus waves near the rockey headland.

Circle the word that has the nearest meaning to the underlined word.

9. Ted's not a very <u>competent</u> swimmer.

   (a) fit   (b) capable   (c) gifted   (d) inadequate

10. When will the King <u>abdicate</u> from his throne?

   (a) resign   (b) defend   (c) appoint   (d) cancel

Circle the correct word in brackets.

11. All the equipment was (pact / packed) into the cupboards.

12. There was a brilliant (lightening / lightning) strike behind the clubhouse.

Grammar and Punctuation

13. Write the plural forms of the nouns underlined.

I have a good <u>supply</u> of <u>wool</u> to complete the <u>cargo</u>.

14. Punctuate and capitalise this sentence.

its important for the rescuer to kneel beside the victims side then perform cpr if need be

Number and Algebra

1. Here is a large number: 734 752. For the second 7 to have the same value as the first 7, what must be done with it? _____

2. Write one point oh two five billion in digits.

   _____

3. Round off the number 11.7187:
   (a) to the nearest tenth _____
   (b) to the nearest thousandth _____

4. Arrange in descending order of magnitude.
   $\frac{7}{9}, \frac{1}{3}, \frac{5}{6}, \frac{1}{2}, \frac{1}{9}$ _____

5. What decimal is 4 minutes 30 seconds of 6 minutes? _____

6. $127 \times 27 + 38 \times 42 - 7 \times 39$ _____

7. Coins were collected for charity: 38 five-cent coins, 49 ten-cent coins, 58 fifty-cent coins and 11 two-dollar coins. What was the total value of the donated coins? _____

8. What is the difference between $4\frac{5}{16}$ and $2\frac{1}{2}$? _____

9. A motorist is allowed a 10% discount on tyres marked at $247.20 each. What will the motorist pay for four new tyres? _____

10. In a rectangle, the ratio of length to width is $4:3$. If the perimeter is 14 cm, what is the length of the rectangle? _____

11. There are x items in a box. y boxes are packed into each carton. There are z cartons on the pallet. The algebraic expression to find the number of items on the pallet is:
    (a) $(x + y)z$ (b) $x + y + z$
    (c) $\frac{x + y}{z}$ (d) $x \times y \times z$
    Circle the correct one.

12. When $x = 4$ and $y = 3$, what is the value of $4x + 2y$? _____

13. What is the missing number? _____
    $4 \times \square + 2 = 26$

14. Join the sets of co-ordinates and state which type of figure is drawn.
    $(1, 3), (3, 6), (5, 3), (3, 0)$

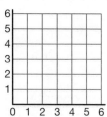

_____

Measurement and Space

15. What % of 4 t is 800 kg? _____

16. Underline the correct answer. 0.3 m means:
    3 km   3 m   3 cm   3 mm   30 cm   30 mm

17. A parallelogram has an area of 72 cm². If the height is 9 cm what is the length of the base? _____

18. Capacity of a rectangular prism = 6 L, length = 20 cm, width = 30 cm, depth = _____ cm.

19. Name this shape.

_____

20. $\angle QWT = \angle UXR$. True or false?

    _____

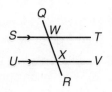

Statistics and Probability

21. A normal dice is rolled 5 times and each time the result is odd. What is the probability that on the sixth roll the result is even?

    _____

22. 17, 38, 24, 15, 16, 51, 32, 12, 27, 22, 16, 19, 43
    Arrange these scores in descending order. Circle the median.

    _____

Film review

Nicki—

Here's the goss—gargantuan news! Went and saw the film 'Secret Messages'. Fabuloso movie, one of the best I've ever seen! It's about aliens invading Earth and stealing the thoughts from people's brains. Some parts were kinda spooky, especially the bit where Arna is taken hostage aboard the spaceship Zeron. She manages to escape by stowing away on the ship when they go back to Earth to get more brains. The star is Al Matilda, and his protruding nose and weird ears make him perfect for the role. The special effects were out of this world (excuse the pun!); you have to see them to believe them. Maybe two and a half hours is a bit long but for eight bucks I'm not complaining. You gotta go see it. I'm willing to see it twice! I'm free this arvo …

Naku-naku (alien talk for see you),   Jordan

Jordan's Film Review Guide

Excellent, Fabuloso!	☆☆☆☆☆
Kinda cool!	☆☆☆☆
All right	☆☆☆
Some hope!	☆☆
Down 'n Out	☆

Reading and Comprehension

1. A *pun* is
(a) similar to a preposition.
(b) a profound English expression.
(c) the humorous use of words with a double meaning.
(d) a suitable facial expression.

2. Jordan believes the movie is
(a) interesting.   (b) excellent.
(c) one of the best.   (d) far too long.

3. What star rating would Jordan give 'Secret Messages'?

_____

4. With whom does Jordan want to see the movie again?

_____

5. What is meant by the term 'special effects' as applied to movies?

_____

6. Arrange in chronological order.
(a) Arna is taken hostage.   _____
(b) Aliens begin stealing thoughts.   _____
(c) Arna stows away on a ship
     back to Earth.   _____
(d) Aliens begin invading Earth.   _____

Spelling and Vocabulary

Rewrite the misspelt words.

7. Peter boastid that he was capible of doing much better.

_____

8. They were especialy sorry they missed the opening momants of the film.

_____

Circle the word that has the nearest meaning to the underlined word.

9. There was an <u>appalling</u> display of violence in that video.
(a) safe   (b) secure   (c) abolishing   (d) shocking

10. Al Matilda is an <u>eminent</u> actor in film.
(a) obscure   (b) well-known
(c) unknown   (d) eccentric

Circle the correct word in brackets.

11. There was a (sleight / slight) flaw in the piece of developed film.

12. (There / Their / They're) aren't any programs left madam.

Grammar and Punctuation

13. Fill in the blanks using the correct form of the adjective in brackets.
(a) Which are the _____ , prawns or oysters? (dear)
(b) My brothers are _____ than me. (young)

14. Punctuate and capitalise this sentence.

mrs b c whiteman gave mr t c smithers an award for best playwright

_____

Number and Algebra

1. The number 4 has only three factors: 1, 2 and 4. Find three other numbers less than 50 that also only have three factors. _____

2. $7 \times 10^2 + 8 \times 10^6 + 9 \times 10^0 + 3 \times 10^4 + 8 \times 10^9 + 1 \times 10^7$. Write in standard form. _____

3. Arrange these fractions in ascending order: 32%, $\frac{1}{3}$, 0.25, six twentieths, 19 hundredths _____

4. Convert these mixed numbers to improper fractions.
   $2\frac{3}{5}$ _____ $5\frac{7}{12}$ _____ $6\frac{7}{10}$ _____

5. Tim's bank balance moves from a debit of $20 to a debit of $5. Has he:
   (a) deposited money or
   (b) withdrawn money? _____

6. What is the sum of $\frac{4}{5}$ of 9.75 t and $\frac{3}{4}$ of 11.25 t? _____

7. $19\,583.6 - 9\,995.07 = $ _____

8. Find the sum of $5\frac{5}{6}$ and $2\frac{1}{5}$. _____

9. A car priced at $64\,000 is discounted by 10%. What is the new price? _____

10. Express the first quantity as a ratio of the second.
    (a) 9 mm : 2.7 cm _____
    (b) 60 litres : 12 000 mL _____

11. If $a = 8$ and $b = 4$, what is the quotient when a is divided by b? _____

12. What is $\frac{1}{3}$ of $6ab$? _____

13. The triangle XYZ is rotated a quarter turn in an anticlockwise direction about the vertex Z.

    What is the location of the image of X?

    _____

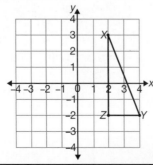

14. Prove by substitution that $b \div (x + 3y)$ is the same as $\frac{b}{x + 3y}$ (suggest $b = 24$, $x = 5$ and $y = 1$). ☐ True ☐ False

Measurement and Space

15. Express these analog times as 24-hour times.
    (a) twenty-seven minutes past 4 in the morning _____
    (b) thirty-nine minutes to 7 in the evening _____

16. Use your calculator to multiply 43.216 metres by 28 and express your answer in kilometres. _____

17. What is the area of the shaded section? _____

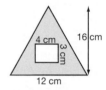

18. Write the liquid volume in:
    (a) L _____
    (b) mL _____

19. Lines have been drawn in these two triangles. How many triangles can you find in each of the figures? _____ _____

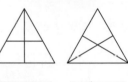

20. In this diagram you are given only two angles.
    (a) Name the 6 unknown angles.

    _____

    (b) Find their sizes.

    _____

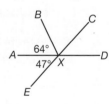

Statistics and Probability

21. Seven green cards and three red cards are placed in a box. When four green cards are taken out and not returned, what is the probability of drawing a red card from the remaining cards? _____

22. Here are six results in a class quiz.

    8   9   6   8   9   8

    What is the mode? _____

Weaties Breakfast Cereal

Nutrition information
Servings per package: 10
Serving size: 30 g (1 metric cup)

	Per 30 g serve	Per 100 g
Energy	456 kJ	1520 kJ
Protein	3.8 g	12.6 g
Fat	2.25 g	7.5 g
Carbohydrate		
—total	20.15 g	67.1 g
—sugars	6.25 g	20.8 g
Dietary fibre	3.75 g	12.5 g
—insoluble	2.65 g	8.8 g
—soluble	1.1 g	3.6 g
Sodium	10 mg	33.3 mg
Potassium	185 mg	616.6 mg

Vitamin and mineral information

* % RDI	per serve
Thiamine (Vit. B1)	25
Riboflavin (Vit. B2)	12.5
Niacin	12.5
Iron	12.5

* Australian recommended dietary intake

Reading and Comprehension

1. How many grams of fat are there in an average serve of Weaties?
   (a) 2.25 g
   (b) 30 g
   (c) 456 kJ
   (d) 7.5 g

2. What is the net mass of the Weaties Cereal?
   (a) 30 g
   (b) 300 g
   (c) 100 g
   (d) none of the above

3. Which word in the table means 'incapable of being dissolved'?
   _____

4. Which is the correct abbreviation for kilojoule?
   _____

5. Why is it important that food packaging displays nutritional information?
   _____

6. True or false?
   It can be inferred from the table that both thiamine and riboflavin are minerals.
   _____

Spelling and Vocabulary

Rewrite the misspelt words.

7. She applyed for the position of Principle at our school.
   _____

8. Is the data corectly listed in the directorey?
   _____

Circle the word that has the nearest meaning to the underlined word.

9. We worked under such <u>adverse</u> conditions.
   (a) favourable   (b) fortunate
   (c) lucky   (d) hostile

10. The criminal continued to <u>elude</u> police.
    (a) assist   (b) accompany
    (c) evade   (d) oppose

Circle the correct word in brackets.

11. She had a short (laps / lapse) in concentration.

12. This cereal has a (grater / greater) fat content than the other.

Grammar and Punctuation

13. Complete the sentence with a clause containing a proper noun.
    The teacher thanked _____

14. Punctuate and capitalise this sentence.
    we didnt catch a single fish john complained as he took off his muddy black gumboots
    _____
    _____

Number and Algebra

1. Complete:

$a =$	1	2	3	4	5
$a^2 + a =$					

2. Rewrite as a single number:
4 000 000 000 + 27 000 000 + 700 000 + 6000 + 900 + 14

_____

3. (a) When two positive numbers are added the answer is _____.

(b) The sum of two negative numbers is a _____ number.

(c) The sum of a negative and a positive number is always a negative.
☐ True ☐ False

4. What is $\frac{5}{9}$ of 0.75 of an hour in minutes? _____

5. -6 is a intervals left of -2. Find a. _____

6. $800\,000 - 348\,009 =$ _____

7. $50 \div 11 = 4.\dot{5}\dot{4}$
(a) $60 \div 11 =$ _____
(b) $70 \div 11 =$ _____

8. $5\frac{5}{12} + 3\frac{1}{6} - 4\frac{1}{9} =$ _____

9. What percentage is 50c of $2? _____

10. Express the ratio in its simplest form.
1.2 m : 1.92 m _____

11. A vehicle travels 160 kilometres on y litres of fuel. How far would it go on z litres at the same rate? _____

12. Find the numerical value of $2x^2 + x$ if $x = 4$. _____

13. Solve $12 - 2a = 6$. _____

14. The points $A(-3, 5)$ and $B(-3, -1)$ are plotted on a cartesian plane. What are the coordinates of the point in the middle of A and B?

_____

Measurement and Space

15. Here is a calendar. On what day will the first of July fall?

MAY

S	M	T	W	T	F	S
			1	2	3	4
5	6	7	8	9	10	11
12	13	14	15	16	17	18
19	20	21	22	23	24	25
16	27	28	29	30	31	

_____

16. A regular octagonal piece of card has a perimeter of 1.728 metres. How long is each side? _____

17. From a rectangular piece of cardboard 36 cm long and 24 cm wide, I cut out a triangle with a base of 24 cm and a perpendicular height of 22 cm. What area of the sheet remains? _____

18. A box is 27 cm long, 25 cm wide and 60 mm deep. What is its volume in cubic centimetres? _____

19. Name the 3D shape that has 2 edges, 3 faces, no apex and no corners. _____

20. What are the sizes of the following angles?
(a) $AXY =$ _____
(b) $EYB =$ _____
(c) $DYF =$ _____

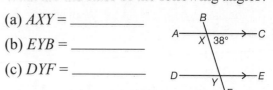

Statistics and Probability

21. A bag contains 18 coloured sticks. How many sticks are blue if the probability of drawing a blue one is $\frac{1}{3}$? _____

22. Here are five scores: 8, 9, 12, 4, ☐.
If the mean is 7, what is the missing score? _____

Letter of complaint

Cr Albert Jones   John J Citizen
Member for Smithville   3G Smith St
PO Box 999   Smithville Qld 4999
Smithville Qld 4999   (07) 3555 5555

Dear Sir

Safety Issue—Lack of footpath along
        12–14 Smith St. Smithville

I would like to bring to your attention the state of the footpath at the above location. Presently, there is a rough dirt section of about 40 metres which remains unsealed on this path. As a regular user of the path, I have to walk onto the roadway to negotiate this hazard.

It is difficult to use the other side of the road, as it is separated by a median strip and guard rail. I have seen joggers, pedestrians and mothers pushing strollers go directly onto the roadway to negotiate the area. As Smith Street is an arterial road, these detours can be quite dangerous.

I submit that this section requires sealing as a matter of urgency, and request your earliest attention to this matter.

Yours Faithfully   _JCitizen_

Reading and Comprehension

1. Letters of complaint should be treated as
   (a) a nuisance.
   (b) a way of bringing something of concern to someone's attention.
   (c) something to be ignored.
   (d) unnecessary paperwork that wastes people's time.

2. An arterial road
   (a) is always a dual carriageway.
   (b) is like a side street.
   (c) is a major channel or route.
   (d) pertains to trucks only.

3. Who is Albert Jones?

   _____

4. Why doesn't Mr Citizen use the other side of the road?

   _____

5. In your own words, why does the partially missing footpath represent a safety hazard?

   _____

6. Which of these statements is **not** implied or stated in the letter?
   (a) John Citizen uses the footpath regularly.
   (b) Smith Street is a busy road.
   (c) Mr Jones is the Member for Smithville.
   (d) John Citizen is an original Smith Street resident.

Spelling and Vocabulary

Rewrite the misspelt words.

7. Thomas keeps complaning about his assinments and homework.

   _____

8. Many of the letters recieved by the council were adressed to the local Member.

   _____

Circle the word that has the nearest meaning to the underlined word.

9. We arrived at the office underlined{unannounced}.
   (a) courteously   (b) yesterday
   (c) uncertainly   (d) unexpectedly

10. He is such a underlined{zealous} student.
    (a) jealous   (b) lazy   (c) enthusiastic   (d) apathetic

Circle the correct word in brackets

11. People were held as (captors / captives) during the war.

12. The (corps / corpse) was taken to the morgue.

Grammar and Punctuation

13. Add the past participle of _break_ to complete the sentence.

    _____ by the strong wind the branch fell to the ground.

14. Punctuate and capitalise this sentence.
    did you collect the babies blankets and put them in their cots

    _____

Number and Algebra

1. Continue this series.
   13 787 150, 13 787 300, 13 787 450,

   _____, _____, _____

2. What number is 100 more
   than negative 67? _____
   What number is 1000 more
   than −23? _____

3. Calculate the highest common
   factors of 72 and 96. _____

4. Rewrite these decimals as simplified fractions:
   0.4, 0.8, 0.005, 0.0125 _____

5. Zero lies midway between x and −3.
   Find x on the number line. _____

   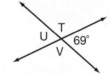

6. Camping chairs are on sale for $49.85.
   What is the cost of half a dozen
   of these chairs? _____
   What remains from $400
   after the purchase? _____

7. Subtract 395c from $6.50. _____

8. Simplify:
   $\frac{5}{7} \times \left(\frac{3}{4} \div \frac{1}{8}\right)$ _____

9. A small second-hand car was sold for $3520.
   The agent received $7\frac{1}{2}\%$ commission on the
   sale. What did the seller receive? _____

10. In a school the ratio of students to staff is 23 : 1.
    If there are 20 staff, how many students are
    enrolled at the school? _____

11. If $x = 7$, what is the value of this algebraic
    expression? $6(x + x^2 − 5)$ is _____.

12. How many pieces of steel each measuring
    x centimetres can be cut from a steel rod
    m metres long? _____

13. Simplify $2 − 4a − 6 − 3a$. _____

14. Solve $\frac{x + 6}{2} = 11$. _____

Measurement and Space

15. One tonne of packing material costs $1110.
    How much per kilogram is this? _____

16. A family began travelling to their camping
    site. It was exactly 148.8 km away. When they
    had covered five-eighths of the distance,
    how far had they still to go? _____

17. What is the area of the shaded portion?

    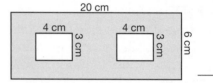

    _____

18. A cubical fish tank has an edge of 3.2 m.
    What volume of water
    will it be able to hold? _____

19. A line is drawn to cut a regular hexagon into
    an isosceles triangle and a _____.

20. Give the measure of angle T.

    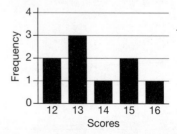

    _____

Statistics and Probability

21. What is the probability of drawing an ace
    from a set of playing cards?

    _____

22. A set of scores is used to draw a histogram.
    What is the mode of the scores?

    _____

Shark Alert!

Unwary swimmers have been exposed to the threat of shark attack during the past couple of months at one of our most popular beaches. Damage to protective nets has not been repaired. The nylon nets have several tears in them and local resident Mrs Betty Appleby said regular beachgoers are at great risk when swimming there.

The local Municipal Council Alderman, Mr Joe Kouton, raised concerns at a recent council meeting. 'I'm very angry that damaged nets have been left in place. It's frightening and irresponsible,' he said. 'To make matters worse, no warning signs have been erected. One thing's for sure, I'm not swimming there until the nets have been repaired.'

A spokesperson for Outer-Reef Safety Nets denied that the damage was serious. She indicated that the high seas and severe wind squalls had hampered attempts to make repairs. It is expected that all nets will be in first-class condition by next weekend.

Reading and Comprehension

1. What is the news article highlighting?
    (a) the potential danger to beachgoers
    (b) the damage to the shark nets
    (c) the local residents' concerns
    (d) all of the above

2. Which of the following statements is clearly defined in the story?
    (a) Mrs Appleby is a regular swimmer at the beach.
    (b) There have been shark attacks because of the net damage.
    (c) Net damage has not been repaired.
    (d) The Council is responsible for fixing the net.

3. Which forum did the Alderman choose to voice his concerns?

    _____

4. What resolution did the Alderman make?

    _____

5. What feelings would you expect regular beach-goers to have after reading the article?

    _____

6. Were there two opposing views expressed in the article? If so, what were they?

    _____

    _____

Spelling and Vocabulary

Rewrite the misspelt words.

7. The councel was embarrased about the news artical.

    _____

8. Make-up your own opinyon about the headline and the story.

    _____

Circle the word that has the nearest meaning to the underlined word.

9. We will <u>interrupt</u> this meeting for lunch.
    (a) maintain (b) adjourn (c) prolong (d) intervene

10. Clearly, the swimmer was <u>distressed</u>.
    (a) contented   (b) suffering
    (c) anxious   (d) uncomfortable

Circle the correct word in brackets.

11. Dad and I (checked / chequed) the net this morning.

12. (Lie / Lay) this rope along the bottom of the boat.

Grammar and Punctuation

13. Use *mending the nets* as a phrase in a suitable sentence.

    _____

    _____

14. Punctuate and capitalise this sentence.

    why wasnt action taken any sooner demanded mr wilson

    _____

    _____

Number and Algebra

1. Is this statement correct? The sum of a positive and a negative number is always less than zero. ☐ True ☐ False

2. What is the value of $(-1)^3 - (-1)^2$? _____

3. Write 30 and one thousand, four hundred and forty-seven ten thousandths as a decimal. _____

4. Solve. $\frac{5}{7} \times \frac{3}{8} + 1\frac{3}{7} =$ _____

5. A substance has a freezing point of $-114\ °C$. Its boiling point is $78\ °C$. What is the difference between these two temperatures? _____

6. There were 728 people at a concert. One-quarter were men, one-half were women and the remainder were children. How many children were present? _____

7. Subtract the least of these from the greatest. $\frac{1}{3}$ of $83.04, $\frac{1}{4}$ of $107.04, $\frac{1}{2}$ of $56.28 _____

8. From the sum of $\frac{2}{3}$ and three-quarters, take 0.25. _____

9. What is the difference between 120% of $395 and $7\frac{1}{2}$% of $15.60? _____

10. Erin and Evan share prize money in the ratio of 3 : 4. If Erin has $240, how much money has Evan? _____

11. $2xy \times 3x \times 4y$ can be written more simply as _____.

12. Expand $-8 (x^2 + 3)$. _____

13. Locate these co-ordinates on the grid, then join them.

(2, 3), (2, 8), (7, 8), (8, 2)

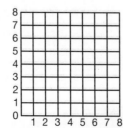

14. If $A = \frac{1}{2}xy$, what is the value of A when $x = 18$ and $y = 14$? _____

Measurement and Space

15. Convert the following:
(a) 4.163 t into kilograms _____
(b) 5127 g into kilograms _____

16. Write the correct measures.
5.7 cm = 5 _____ 7 _____ = 57 _____

17. A road is 60 metres long. The footpath on either side is 2.5 m wide. What is the total area of the footpaths? _____

18. Which container would hold the greater amount of liquid? _____
(a) a cube with a side of 5 cm
(b) a rectangular prism with dimensions 6 cm, 4 cm and 2 cm

19. What shape is the cross-section of this figure? _____

20. Find the measure of angle QRS. _____

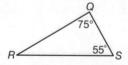

Statistics and Probability

21. Here is a list of a cricketer's scores: 16, 38, 8, 26, 0, 28, 20 and 72. Calculate the mean of these scores. _____

22. The stem-and-leaf plot shows the ages of people living in a retirement village. What is the range of the ages?

Stem	Leaf
6	26
7	35899
8	46668
9	7

_____

How much do we waste?
How much do we recycle?

	Paper/cardboard	Glass	Steel
Used in making	Wrapping, writing paper, books, containers	Bottles, jars	Cars, buses, trains, ships, buildings, bridges, tools, cans, household equipment
Type of waste	Household, industrial and commercial	Household, industrial	Household, industrial
Amount used	150 kg	57 kg	16 kg in packaging
Amount recycled from all sources	53 kg	10 kg	80 kg (mostly from industry)
Amount recycled from household waste	14 kg	Almost 10 kg	Very small amount
How much more could be recycled	over 63 kg	28–45 kg	9–16 kg from household rubbish

Note: all amounts are per person/year.

From *What a Waste!* by Stephen Jones

Reading and Comprehension

1. The amount of glass recycled from household waste per person per year is
   (a) 10 kg.   (b) 14 kg.
   (c) less than 10%.   (d) almost 10 kg.

2. How much more steel could be recycled per person/year?
   (a) no figures available (b) 28–45 kg
   (c) 9–16 kg   (d) 80 kg

3. Which are the two most common environments in which waste is generated?

4. According to the table, which item(s) is (are) most used per person per year?

5. Why do you think that paper and cardboard show the best recycling figures?

6. What conclusion can be drawn from the amount of all items recycled from all sources, compared to the amount of all items used?

Spelling and Vocabulary

Rewrite the misspelt words.

7. Most plastic pakaging is diposed of as garbage.

8. Food scrapes and garden wast can be used as compost.

Circle the word that has the nearest meaning to the underlined word.

9. Practising recycling requires discipline.
   (a) self-control   (b) organisation
   (c) focus   (d) disguise

10. Try not to accumulate too much garbage.
    (a) scatter (b) amass (c) separate (d) devote

Circle the correct word in brackets.

11. The local (counsel / council) introduced recycling.

12. A (draft / draught) of cold air could be felt in the corridor.

Grammar and Punctuation

13. Change this sentence into passive voice.
    Several of the workers removed the waste.

14. Punctuate and capitalise this text.
    use bags baskets and boxes to carry shopping purchases avoid collecting plastic bags

Number and Algebra

1. (a) Write three billion, one hundred and seven million, three hundred and forty-three. _____

   (b) Write in words 101.101. _____

2. Complete:

$a =$	2	4	6	8	10
$x^3 + 4 =$					

3. $2^6 \div 2^2 = 2^3$

   If this statement is incorrect, then alter the right-hand side of the equation to make it true. _____

4. Match these fractions.

47%	0.32
32%	0.47
50%	$\frac{1}{100}$
1%	$\frac{27}{10}$
270%	0.5

5. Graph these fractions on the number line.

   $\dfrac{16}{3}, \dfrac{12}{3}, \dfrac{15}{3}, \dfrac{9}{3}, \dfrac{6}{3}$

   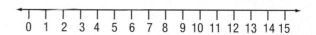

6. $(4683 - 2797) \times 16 =$ _____

7. The contents of 28 cartons each containing 264 toys were repacked into boxes each containing 66 toys. How many additional boxes were needed? _____

8. From the sum of $2\frac{1}{3}$ and $5\frac{5}{12}$, subtract $3\frac{1}{3}$.
   The answer is _____.

9. Charlotte is paid $1420 per week. She is to receive a pay rise of 2%.
   What will be Charlotte's new pay? _____

10. Container A holds 1250 mL and B contains 1.6 L.
    Express the ratio of the contents of $B:A$ in the simplest term. _____

11. Create an algebraic expression that means
    the product of x^2 and y^2 divided by 3. _____

12. Verify that this equation $4x + (x^3 - 100) = 45$ is correct by substituting 5 for x.
    The question is ☐ correct ☐ incorrect.

13. If $a = 3$, $b = 4$ and $c = 2$, find the value of $ab - c$. _____

14. Mark these co-ordinates on the grid.

A(4, 1), B(6, 2), C(2, 4), D(1, 5)

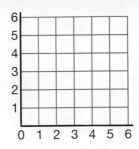

Measurement and Space

15. How many kilograms are there in 17.013 tonnes? _____

16. 3750 metres is written as _____ kilometres.

17. A triangular pennant has a base of 30 cm and a perpendicular height of 45 cm. What is the total area of six of these pennants? _____

18. How many medicine glasses holding 50 mL can be poured from a 1.75-L bottle of syrup? _____

19. A 2D shape does not have: ☐ length   ☐ depth   ☐ width

20. Five minutes on a clock face shows an angle of _____° between the hands.

Statistics and Probability

21. The arrow is spun on the spinner.

What is the probability that the number is an odd number greater than 4?

_____

22. The table shows the number of times a group of adults have visited a doctor in the past 6 months.

Number of visits	Number of people
0	5
1	9
2	11
3	6

Find:

(a) mode   _____

(b) range   _____

(c) median   _____

Radio news

Although most people say they get their news from television, when some event is occurring, people usually first turn on the radio for information.

This is so for several reasons: radio is more accessible than the other media; its news bulletins are more frequent; radio news journalists are usually able to get to the scene of an event more quickly and get the news onto the airwaves sooner; and the radio can involve its listeners in the news more easily. Radio is, then, a valuable news source.

Radio is more accessible for a number of reasons. One is that every home, almost every car and a large number of workplaces have one. This means that it is easy to find a radio and turn it on. Another is that some radios are so small it is possible to carry one in a pocket and listen to it whenever you want. Finally, you can listen to the radio while you do other things. It does not matter if you are in bed or at the beach, driving a car or camping in the country, walking around the street or working in the backyard, radio news is accessible.

While newspapers and television channels usually have only one main edition each day, radio news programs are broadcast frequently. Radio stations have a news bulletin at least every hour. This means that radio can report on events as they happen and update the reports as more information is gathered.

Radio can often be first with the news because radio journalists need to carry little equipment. A notebook and a hand-held tape-recorder is much easier to load, carry and set up than the equipment television journalists need. This means radio journalists can quickly arrive at an event. Unlike the other two media, radio journalists can go to air quickly, simply by telephoning their station or by using a small radio handset, much like a walkie-talkie.

Radio news can involve listeners more effectively than the other media. It can seek opinions, questions, comments and further information through talkback radio. It can also abandon all its other programs to concentrate on an important story and to provide a community service. A good example is the way radio news responded to the Ash Wednesday bushfires in 1983.

In February 1983 bushfires erupted across southern Australia from Adelaide to Melbourne. Flames roared through bushland, across farms and through towns to the edge of the big cities, destroying all before them. Thousands of farm and native animals were burnt to death. People fleeing the fires huddled together in halls, schools and on beaches. Seventy-two people died. Many more became separated from friends and family.

As the wind carried ashes from the fires over the city, people turned to their radios for information about the extent of the fires and the damage, the safety of friends and relatives, and where it was safe to go. Radio stations, especially 3AW in Melbourne, sent journalists to the main fire areas.

From *Shaping the News* by John Fitzgerald

Reading and Comprehension

1. Radio news is usually the first choice for people because
   (a) TV stations do not have sufficient resources.
   (b) TV stations only have 6:00 pm news programs.
   (c) radio coverage is more accurate.
   (d) radio news is more accessible.

2. Radio journalists can get to air quickly because
   (a) they work more efficiently than TV reporters.
   (b) they realise the importance of on-the-spot reporting.
   (c) they use limited equipment.
   (d) they are in competition with each other.

3. Radio news is more convenient because
   (a) radios are small and portable.
   (b) news updates can be reported at any time.
   (c) you can listen to the radio while doing other things.
   (d) all of the above

4. During which crisis did radio provide an especially valuable community service?

   _____

   _____

5. How was radio station 3AW able to provide helpful assistance?

   _____

   _____

   _____

6. What is the author's intention?
   (a) to detail the progress of the bushfire
   (b) to convince people to disregard TV news
   (c) to explain why radio news is particularly useful
   (d) to praise radio journalists

Spelling and Vocabulary

Rewrite the misspelt words.

7. The work of radio journelists provides a valueable community service.

   _____

8. The reporter said that there was absolutely nothing that could be done to prevent his home from being distroyed.

   _____

Circle the word that has the nearest meaning to the underlined word.

9. She said that the radio was more underline{accessible}.
   (a) reliable
   (b) responsible
   (c) available
   (d) accommodating

10. The response that he made was the correct one.
    (a) resumption
    (b) restriction
    (c) reaction
    (d) resident

Circle the correct word in brackets.

11. Radio is indeed a valuable news (sauce / source).

12. The journalist can concentrate on a good (storey / story).

Grammar and Punctuation

13. Of what word is *best* the superlative adjective?

    _____

14. Punctuate and capitalise this sentence.

    why asked the girl did you not even bother to have the equipment repaired

    _____

    _____

    _____

Mathematics

Number and Algebra

1. (=, <, >)
    Use the correct sign to complete the following:
    (a) 7^3 _____ 4^4 (b) 9^3 _____ 3^6

2. $6.5079 = 1 \times 10^{\square} + 6 \times \_\_^0 + \frac{5}{10^{\square}} + \frac{9}{10^{\square}} + \frac{9}{10^{\square}}$

3. Round 16.8742 to the nearest:
    (a) tenth   _____
    (b) thousandth   _____
    (c) ten   _____

4. Rearrange these recurring decimal numbers so that they are in ascending order.

    $$0.6, \text{ one-third}, \frac{5}{11}, \frac{4}{9}$$

    _____

5. $(7.031 - 2.387) \times 4.3$ _____

6. What is 983 more than 12 984?   _____

7. By how much is 20.65 greater than 15.983?   _____

8. How many times is $\frac{3}{10}$ contained in $1\frac{4}{5}$?   _____

9. Mabel is driving a 200-km distance between two cities. She has already driven 40 km. What percentage of the total distance has she yet to drive?   _____

10. Share $1303.68 between A and B in the ratio of 4:3.

    A _____ B _____

11. l^4 is the same as $l \times 4$ / $l + l + l + l$ / $l \times l \times l \times l$ / $4l$.   Circle the correct one.

12. Mark the points.
    A(1, 3)
    B(–2, –4)
    C(–1, 4)
    D(–3, 5)

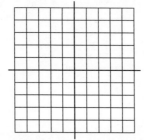

13. To find the area of a rectangle with sides of x and y, is the algebraic expression $x + y$, $x - y$, $\frac{x}{y}$ or xy? Circle the correct one.

14. Solve the equation $2a - 0.5 = 3.5$.   _____

Measurement and Space

15. What decimal is 750 kg of a tonne?   _____

16. There are _____ mm in 4.68 m.

17. Supply the missing dimensions of this triangle: base 70 cm, area 1330 cm², perpendicular height   _____

18. A rectangular prism has dimensions 5 cm, 2 cm and 2 cm. How many times could it be emptied into a cubic container with a side of 10 cm?   _____

19. What is the approximate ratio of a diameter of a circle to the circumference of the same circle?   _____

20. What are the sizes of the following angles?
    (a) BDE = _____
    (b) FDH = _____
    (c) EHG = _____

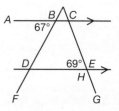

Statistics and Probability

21. A bag contains 4 red balls, 5 green balls and 3 blue balls. A ball is chosen at random. What is the probability that it is **not** green?

    _____

22. Here is a stem-and-leaf plot.

Stem	Leaf
5	47
6	2267
7	04
8	3
9	04

What is the median?

    _____

Andy's gone with cattle

Our Andy's gone with cattle now—
Our hearts are out of order—
With drought he's gone to battle now
Across the Queensland border.

He's left us in dejection now;
Our thoughts with him are roving;
It's dull on this selection now,
Since Andy went a-droving.

Who now shall wear the cheerful face
In times when things are slackest?
And who shall whistle round the place
When Fortune frowns her blackest?

Oh, who shall cheek the squatter now
When he comes round us snarling?
His tongue is growing hotter now
Since Andy crossed the Darling.

Henry Lawson

Reading and Comprehension

1. Where has Andy gone?
   (a) across the Darling
   (b) across the Queensland border
   (c) the next selection
   (d) both (a) and (b)
   (e) both (a) and (c)

2. Who or what has Andy gone with?
   (a) the rude squatter
   (b) black Fortune
   (c) cattle
   (d) a rover

3. In the second verse what is meant by a *selection*?

   _____

4. Who was causing a problem?

   _____

5. Describe the feelings of the people in the poem because of Andy's departure.

   _____

   _____

6. Why did everyone like to have Andy around?

   _____

   _____

Spelling and Vocabulary

Rewrite the misspelt words.

7. The extract is part of a balad which was originaly a story set to music.

   _____

8. He looked slightley built alongside many of his opponnents.

   _____

Circle the word that has the nearest meaning to the underlined word.

9. My grandma is sprightly for a woman of ninety-two.
   (a) lifeless   (b) sluggish
   (c) lively   (d) springy

10. Traditionally, governments are seen as being cautious.
    (a) stable   (b) jaunty
    (c) serious   (d) conservative

Circle the correct word in brackets.

11. The rain will (effect / affect) our camping plans for the weekend.

12. The (stationery / stationary) engine was used to pump water to the fish tank.

Grammar and Punctuation

13. Circle the pronouns in this sentence.

    Underline the word the adjective clause refers to.
    I read the poem which you suggested.

14. Write in indirect speech.

    'I have been there before,' he said.

    _____

    _____

Number and Algebra

1. Write the number that is ten thousand more than 384 725. _____
   Write the number that is one hundred thousand more than 3 997 406. _____

2. Place the decimal point so that the 7 is worth $\frac{7}{10^2}$ in 243 752. _____

3. $7 \times 10^4 + 6 \times 10^9 + 3 \times 10^5 + 8 \times 10^1 + 9 \times 10^0$ can be written as the number _____ .

4. Express these improper fractions as mixed numbers.
   (a) $\frac{17}{3}$ _____ (b) $\frac{29}{9}$ _____

5. Which sign ($<$, $=$ or $>$) is the correct one to use in this operation?
   $-3 + -9$ _____ $-5 + -7$

6. $(53 + 96 + 83 + 77 + 56) - (400 \div 20)$
   = _____

7. Add sixty-two thousand, thirty-five tenths, one hundred and eleven thousand and seventy-five hundredths.

   _____

8. $(3\frac{2}{3} + 4\frac{1}{2}) \times (1\frac{2}{3} - \frac{1}{6})$ _____

9. What would be the actual cost of 3 dozen comics at $1.60 each if a discount of 5% is allowed? _____

10. In a triangle the ratio of the sides is $3 : 4 : 5$. If the shortest side is 9 cm, what is the perimeter? _____

11. Express in symbolic form.
    What would I have left out of x if I bought 4 toys at y each? _____

12. Expand $-2(4 - 6w)$. _____

13. If $a = 3$, what is the value of $(2a)^2 - 2a^2$? _____

14. Mark plots the points $A(-1, -3)$ and $B(4, -3)$ on a cartesian plane.
    What is the length of AB? _____

Measurement and Space

15. Find the difference between 0.926 kg and $\frac{9}{10}$ kg. _____

16. 0.67 km = _____ m

17. To find the area of this combined shape, the equation is:

    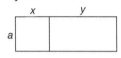

    $a \times x \times y$
    $a(xy)$
    $a(x + y)$
    $\frac{a}{xy}$

    Circle the correct one.

18. A 9-L bucket is half filled with water. Lara pours 120 mL from the bucket. What amount of water remains in the bucket? _____

19. Draw and label TSP which is 37° less than a straight angle. Use the ray as one arm of your angle.

20. Use your protractor to find angle XYZ.

    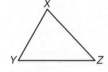

    _____

Statistics and Probability

21. List the four different outcomes when two coins are tossed.

    _____

22. Use the dot plot to find the median. _____

    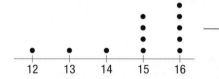

Tabouli

Tabouli is a cracked wheat (burghul) and parsley salad.

Ingredients

1/2 cup burghul
1 cup coarsely chopped Lebanese parsley
    (ordinary parsley will do)
1/8 cup finely chopped mint
1 cup cold water
1/4 cup finely chopped spring onions
1/8 cup olive oil
1 tablespoon lemon juice
1 tomato

Method

1. Put burghul in a container, cover with cold water and allow to soak for at least 30 minutes.
2. Drain burghul into a colander and press it down, to remove all moisture.
3. Place burghul in a large mixing bowl and add the spring onions, mint and parsley.
4. Combine olive oil and lemon juice and add to the salad, tossing well.
5. Dice tomatoes and stir gently into the salad.

Reading and Comprehension

1. Which of the following are vegetables needed to make Tabouli?
   (a) parsley   (b) mint
   (c) spring onions   (d) Lebanese tomatoes

2. Which of the following ingredients are processed?
   (a) cold water   (b) parsley
   (c) tomato   (d) olive oil
   (e) both (a) and (d)

3. How many liquid ingredients are used in this recipe?
   _____

4. What is burghul?
   _____

5. According to the recipe for Tabouli, how much cooking is involved?
   _____

6. Number these instructions in the correct order.
   (a) Remove moisture from burghul.   ____
   (b) Cover burghul with cold water.   ____
   (c) Allow burghul to soak for half an hour. ____
   (d) Combine olive oil and lemon juice.   ____

Spelling and Vocabulary

Rewrite the misspelt words.

7. In the debaiting team, I represanted the affirmative side.
   _____

8. Have you included quototion marks in that factuel text?
   _____

Circle the word that has the nearest meaning to the underlined word.

9. The <u>pivotal</u> point of the service was when they exchanged rings.
   (a) irrelevant   (b) focused
   (c) passive   (d) crucial

10. Your drawing is <u>partially</u> complete.
    (a) totally   (b) partly   (c) almost   (d) entirely

Circle the correct word in brackets.

11. The man (cited / sighted) insanity as his reason for the offence.

12. One of the magistrate's roles is to (meet / mete / meat) out justice.

Grammar and Punctuation

13. State whether the underlined word is a preposition or adverb.

    Tracy jumped <u>over</u>.
    _____

14. Punctuate and capitalise this text.

    what a lovely morning it is val exclaimed lets go for a walk through the botanical gardens
    _____
    _____
    _____

Number and Algebra

1. Find the LCM of the two numbers 16 and 12. _____

2. Complete.

$x =$	1	2	3	4	5
(a) $x^2 =$					
(b) $x^3 =$					

3. Write the lowest common multiple of
  (a) 4, 5, 6 _____
  (b) 2, 7, 8 _____

4. Arrange these common fractions from least to greatest: $\frac{2}{3}$, $\frac{3}{4}$, $\frac{5}{6}$, $\frac{5}{12}$ and $\frac{1}{2}$
  _____

5. A directed number added to its opposite gives zero. ☐ True ☐ False

6. Take 120 952 from 600 000. _____

7. If three cartons of eggs costs $18.25, what is the cost of 18 cartons? _____

8. From $3\frac{1}{7}$ subtract $2\frac{11}{21}$. _____

9. What percentage is 50 cents of $5? _____

10. Cordial was poured into two containers in the ratio of $3:5$. There is 250 mL more in one container than the other. How much is in both containers? _____

11. $4a - 5a - 5a$ _____

12. A table and chair together cost n. The table cost x more than the chair. Show in algebraic form how much the chair cost.
  _____

13. Reflect the triangle about the y–axis.

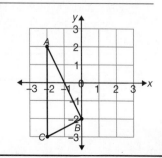

14. What is the value of n? _____
$$\frac{36 - n}{11} = 3$$

Measurement and Space

15. Nick's mass equals $\frac{3}{4}$ of Jenny's mass. Jenny's mass is 64 kg. What is Nick's mass? _____

16. Write 16 km 27 m in metres. _____

17. Find the missing dimension of this square:
  side = _____ m   area = 625 m²

18. 1 L of water = _____ kg = _____ cm³

19. Name the three surfaces that intersect at the point B.

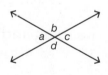

_____

20. (a) $\angle a$ and _____ are vertically opposite angles.
  (b) $\angle d$ and $\angle c$ are _____ angles.
  (c) The sum of $\angle a$, $\angle b$, $\angle c$ and $\angle d$ is _____ .

Statistics and Probability

21. Sectors of the spinner are coloured yellow, blue, red or green.
  What is the probability of spinning red or green?
  _____

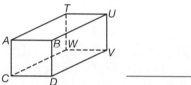

22. Complete the table to match the histogram.

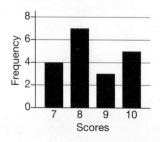

Score	Frequency

The hero returns

Last Saturday the veteran astronaut, John Glenn, returned safely to Earth on the space shuttle Discovery.

Glenn, who is 77 years old, enjoyed his smooth touchdown at Florida's Kennedy Space Center. It was a fitting ending to a nostalgic nine-day orbital odyssey for the astronaut.

On his return, Glenn referred to his famous words from the 1962 space journey 'zero-g and I feel fine'. 'This time it's one-g and I feel fine,' he stated.

Some observers said the mission was designed to gather support for further scientific work, rather than for any particular scientific purpose.

The success of the mission provided an opportunity for many millions of people to think back to the exciting early days of the American–Russian space race. It certainly provided a badly needed boost in support of other space projects, particularly the International Space Station. This project is due to begin later this month.

Reading and Comprehension

1. The terms *zero-g* and *one-g* relate to
   (a) measures of weight (gram).
   (b) the initial for Glenn.
   (c) gravity.
   (d) wind speed.

2. Who was in charge of the space mission?
   (a) the US Space Agency
   (b) John Glenn
   (c) Kennedy Space Center
   (d) the state of Florida

3. Give the meaning of the word *veteran*.

   _____

4. What type of vehicle is a space shuttle?

   _____

   _____

5. What was the underlying reason for sending John Glenn on this mission?

   _____

   _____

6. Explain why the trip was described as a boost for another project.

   _____

   _____

Spelling and Vocabulary

Rewrite the misspelt words.

7. He has an appontment with his solisiter at a quater to eleven.

   _____

8. The migratry habits of some birds are really most remarcable.

   _____

Circle the word that has the nearest meaning to the underlined word.

9. The appropriate <u>ensemble</u> for a barrister in court includes a wig and a black gown.
   (a) ensignature   (b) outfit
   (c) assembly   (d) appearance

10. She was <u>reluctant</u> to finish the work on Saturday.
    (a) favoured (b) reminded (c) prompt (d) unwilling

Circle the correct word in brackets.

11. The animal was (trust / trussed) up in the enclosure.

12. It was difficult for them to (prize / prise) the metal plates apart.

Grammar and Punctuation

13. Underline the adverb in this sentence.

    The students had quickly tidied their desks.

14. Punctuate and capitalise this sentence.

    oddly it took him until 1982 when he was twenty-four to win the australian singles title for the first time

    _____

    _____

    _____

    _____

Mathematics

 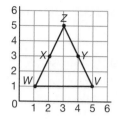

Number and Algebra

1. Use the correct symbol (>, < or =) in this equation.

   $$-32 \times 7 \underline{\qquad} -16 \times 15$$

2. The number 2 413 815 is written. What is the difference between the place value of the two 1s in the number? _____

3. What is the value of one-ninth of -1287? _____

4. What is
   (a) $\frac{4}{5}$ of 5 dozen? _____

   (b) $\frac{9}{11}$ of 104.5 cm? _____

5. A building has a ground floor, 10 levels above that and 4 basements. The lift was on floor 5. Follow its movement. Up 2, down 3, down 5, up 4, down 5, down 1 then up 3. It is now on _____.

6. $4985 + 15\,643 + 8400 + 9597 = \underline{\qquad}$

7. $(51.38 - 37.76) \times 8.2 = \underline{\qquad}$

8. 672 people; $\frac{1}{4}$ men, $\frac{1}{3}$ women and the rest children. How many children are there? _____

9. Jarryd scored 80% in a test of 20 questions, worth 2 marks each. How many questions were correct? _____

10. There are x cats, y birds and z dogs. Show the ratio of cats to dogs to birds. _____

11. Create an algebraic expression which means x plus y divided by the difference between w and z. _____

12. If $x = 9$ and $y = 11$, what is the value of $x^2 + y^2 + xy$? _____

13. What is the average of a, b and c? _____

14. What are the co-ordinates of point Y?

   _____

Measurement and Space

15. An alarm rings every 12 minutes starting at 12 noon. How often will it ring in 5.6 hours? _____

16. How many pieces of ribbon, each 80 cm long, can be cut from a 10 m roll? _____

17. A triangular bandage has a base of 1 m and a perpendicular height of 0.45 m. What is its area? _____

18. The ratio of small to large containers is 2 : 5. Each small container has a capacity of 250 mL and each large container 500 mL. How many containers are required to hold a total of 90 L?

   _____

19. For which solid figure is this a net?

   _____

20. Write the measure of $\angle DIA$.

   _____

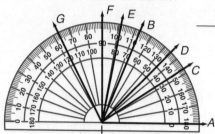

Statistics and Probability

21. A normal dice is rolled. What is the probability that the number shown is **not** odd? _____

22. Here is a set of shoe sizes:
    3, 5, 9, 7, 5, 6, 7, 8, 7, 9, 2, 11, 7, 5, 8, 7, 6, 7, 9, 8, 6, 7, 4, 5, 9, 6, 7, 7, 8, 6.
    Which size is the mode? _____

Kids' editorial
Your say ...

Too many kids are riding their skateboards on public footpaths and it's only a matter of time before an accident will occur. These devices are far too dangerous; maybe governments should think about issuing licences for skateboard riding. I'm an injured pedestrian!
—Glenda Riceton, Mt Carmel

I'm sick and tired of hearing my parents talking about elections. They have seen governments come and go, along with some of their policies and leaders. It seems to me that politicians need to brush up on their communication with the public.
—Dennis Drakos, Calamvale

I strongly disagree with S Pullard (Kids' editorial, 14 February). How much longer are we going to blame the gorgeous red-tailed black cockatoos for destroying crops. Our native birds are so precious and they are suffering because of loss of natural food sources and habitat. This is why our rice crops are being destroyed. Sell them overseas and you might as well sell shares in Australia!!!
—Judy Simmons, Rylstone

Reading and Comprehension

1. What is the red-tailed black cockatoo generally blamed for?
   (a) being greedy
   (b) destroying rice crops
   (c) being sold overseas
   (d) destroying its own habitat

2. The purpose of an editorial is
   (a) for people to share their opinions.
   (b) to bring matters of interest to people's attention.
   (c) to provide a forum for public debate.
   (d) all of the above

3. In this extract, what is meant by *editorial*?

   _____

4. With whose opinion was Judy Simmons disagreeing?

   _____

5. By the tone of the letters, what is the attitude of the three writers?

   _____

6. Fact or opinion? Too many kids are riding their skateboards on public footpaths.

   _____

Spelling and Vocabulary

Rewrite the misspelt words.

7. Conective tissues hold the various struchures of the body together.

   _____

8. Reppetitive pressure on the bones may lead to stress fractures.

   _____

Circle the word that has the nearest meaning to the underlined word.

9. The luxuriant carpet was covered in patterns.
   (a) arid   (b) thin   (c) luxury   (d) opulent

10. The boy on the scooter veered to the right to avoid the kitten.
    (a) tacked   (b) swerved   (c) moved   (d) vaunted

Circle the correct word in brackets.

11. The city was brought under (marshal / martial) law.

12. Could he find the (source / sauce) of the creek?

Grammar and Punctuation

13. Join these sentences by using a clause containing an adverb.

    My grandma sent me a postcard. I have missed her immensely.

    _____

    _____

14. Punctuate and capitalise this text.

    these crops are found in the grantham district wheat oats barley and potatoes

    _____

    _____

Mathematics

Number and Algebra

1. Here are two directed numbers. Place the correct sign ($<$, $>$) between them to make the statement true.

$$-32 \underline{\hspace{1.5cm}} -8.67$$

2. Round 10.0872 to the nearest:

   (a) tenth \underline{\hspace{2cm}}

   (b) hundredth \underline{\hspace{2cm}}

   (c) thousandth \underline{\hspace{2cm}}

3. Complete.

If $y =$	2	5	8	10	20
then $y^2 - y + 5 =$					

4. Change these mixed numbers into improper fractions.

   (a) $7\frac{3}{7}$ \underline{\hspace{2cm}} (b) $6\frac{11}{12}$ \underline{\hspace{2cm}}

5. The correct reading of $+11$ and -11 is positive 11 and negative 11.

   ☐ True ☐ False

6. $27 \times 6750 = \underline{\hspace{2cm}}$

7. Subtract the smallest number from the largest number: 0.967, 0.659, 0.328, 0.999, 0.545 \underline{\hspace{2cm}}

8. Two types of animals: cows and pigs. $\frac{5}{8}$ are cows and 27 are pigs. How many animals are there altogether? \underline{\hspace{2cm}}

9. Full price is $12 650. Discount is 9%. Discounted price is \underline{\hspace{2cm}} .

10. Divide $420 in the ratio $4:3$. \underline{\hspace{2cm}}

11. From the product of b and c subtract the difference between y and z. Show in algebraic form. \underline{\hspace{2cm}}

12. What is the value of x?

   $$\frac{2}{3}x + 7 = 25$$ \underline{\hspace{2cm}}

13. If $a = 3$ and $b = 8$, find the value of $2b - 4a$. \underline{\hspace{2cm}}

14. If x is an odd number, $2x - 1$ is odd.

   ☐ True ☐ False

Measurement and Space

15. In 2023 Charlotte attended school on 197 days. On how many days did she **not** attend? \underline{\hspace{2cm}}

16. Add 4 m 36 cm, 216 mm, 15.7 m and 56 cm. \underline{\hspace{2cm}}

17. The cost of fertilising a paddock is $0.08 per m². Find the cost of fertilising a rectangular paddock measuring 160 m by 100 m.

   \underline{\hspace{2cm}}

18. 0.75 of the contents of a container equals 600 mL. What does the container hold when full? \underline{\hspace{2cm}}

19. Trace in red the side which is opposite vertex G.

20. Consider the interior and exterior angles of triangle BGD.

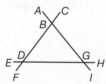

   Name the two angles equal to the sum of BDG and BGD.

   \underline{\hspace{3cm}}

Statistics and Probability

21. In a bag I have 5 red, 7 blue, 8 green and 4 yellow discs. What are the chances of drawing a blue disc? \underline{\hspace{2cm}}

22. What is the mean of the scores in the frequency table? \underline{\hspace{2cm}}

Score	Frequency
10	4
11	7
12	6
13	3

Puppets

A marionette is a full-length, jointed, three-dimensional puppet which is worked by strings or wires which are attached to various parts of the body. Traditionally, marionettes are made of wood, but they can also be made of papier-mâché or plastic. Simple marionettes may have just three strings but some have as many as forty. The strings are tied to a control which is held by the puppeteer.

The main characteristic of the marionette is that it is operated from above. Movement is mainly caused by tilting or rocking the control but when a particular movement is required, the puppeteer pulls on individual strings. The advantage of the marionette is that it can be made to perform almost any human or animal movement. The disadvantage is that the puppeteer must be very skilled. Making a marionette appear lifelike requires much practice.

From *Puppets* by Carole Hooper

Reading and Comprehension

1. Generally speaking, the movement of the puppet is created by
(a) manipulating strings.
(b) the puppeteer's skill.
(c) a plastic control.
(d) wires which are attached to wood.

2. One who manipulates puppets is called
(a) a marionette.   (b) a puppeteer.
(c) a performer.   (d) an operator.

3. Give a definition of a marionette.

_____

4. What is the puppeteer's objective in manipulating the strings of a marionette?

_____

_____

5. What is the difference between a marionette and a puppet?

_____

_____

6. Would the addition of extra strings allow the puppet to be more realistic. If so, explain.

_____

_____

_____

Spelling and Vocabulary

Rewrite the misspelt words.

7. Shado puppets are usualy flat, cut-out figures.

_____

8. The Muppets are a combinaton of hand and rod puppets.

_____

Circle the word that has the nearest meaning to the underlined word.

9. He <u>attached</u> the strings to the control.
(a) secured
(b) wired
(c) assembled
(d) fastened

10. When soldiers are on parade they are never <u>slovenly</u>.
(a) orderly   (b) unsuitable
(c) careless   (d) messy

Circle the correct word in brackets.

11. I got these puppets (off / of / from) my Art teacher.

12. The giggling toddler fell (off / of / from) his seat.

Grammar and Punctuation

13. Underline the subject of the verb *sat*.

On the windowsill sat the toy soldier.

14. Punctuate and capitalise this text.

attach the following pieces eyes mouth hair moustache and ears

_____

_____

_____

Mathematics

Number and Algebra

1. Write this expanded number as a single number. _____
   $3\,000\,000\,000 + 330\,000 + 27\,000 + 2600 + 48$

2. Arrange in ascending order of magnitude.
   $\frac{5}{8}$, 0.701, 4.5, 63%
   _____

3. Complete the pattern. 4, 3.998, 3.996, 3.994,
   _____ , _____

4. Express $\frac{5}{18}$ as a decimal. _____

5.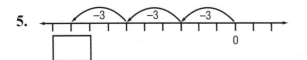

6. Find out how many sevens there are in 1792, then triple it. _____

7. 108 tenths – 956 thousandths = _____

8. An agent sold a car for \$13 500. The agent received $2\frac{1}{2}$% commission. How much less than \$500 did the agent receive? _____

9. Full price \$650. Percent discount 8%.
   Discount _____ .

10. What is the ratio of 250 metres to 4 kilometres? _____

11. By substitution prove that $x \div (y \times z)$ is not equal to $x \div y \times z$. _____

12. How many m millilitre bottles of milk can be filled from n vats each holding y kilolitres. _____

13. Complete the table for the rule $y = 2x - 1$.

x	−1	0	1	2
y				

14. Use the values in the table in question 13 to plot points on the cartesian plane.

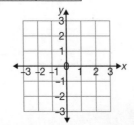

Measurement and Space

15. Complete the following:
    (a) 7.32 t × 8 = _____ kg
    (b) 4.5 t – 520 kg = _____ kg

16. Measure this line to the nearest cm. _____

    ├───────────────────────────────┤

17. A rectangular painting 60 cm by 40 cm has a 3-cm frame around it. What is the area of the frame? _____

18. Which has the greater volume? Circle the correct one.
    a cube with a side of 64 cm
    a rectangular prism 79 cm × 560 mm × 0.52 m

19. A quadrilateral with two pairs of equal sides and only one line of symmetry is a
    _____ .

20. A regular octagon has been split into 6 triangles.

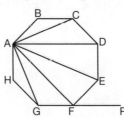

    (a) What is the angle sum of the octagon?
    (b) What is the size of $\angle EFP$? _____

Statistics and Probability

21. Circle the number(s) that **cannot** be the probability of an event: 8%, 0.3, 1.01, $-\frac{1}{2}$

22. Find the median of the scores.

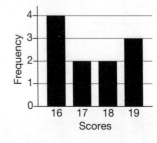

_____

Busy Hands

My nan has busy hands. When she walks in the garden, she plucks off the dead flowers or pulls out a weed or two. In the kitchen she slices, cuts, mixes and stirs to make a delicious meal or cake. Best of all though is when she sits and knits or stitches in her comfortable chair or in a warm sunny spot in the garden.

Sometimes the stitches she uses are intricate and she needs to concentrate to keep the pattern correct but at other times she looks very relaxed and we can chat about all the things I am doing. For my birthday, Nan knitted me a cardigan. She is knitting a vest for Mum and in her work basket is more wool and a pattern for a jumper for my little sister.

Nan does beautiful embroidery too. When I was a baby, she made a beautiful blanket for me. Nan used lots of different threads and stitches to embroider a garden of flowers. When my sister was born, she made another blanket and used lots of other stitches. I still use my blanket to snuggle into when I am watching television.

Nan is teaching me to knit and sew. She patiently untangles my threads, picks up my dropped stitches and fixes my other mistakes. My hands aren't as dexterous as Nan's and my work is not as neat but one day I hope I will be able to make beautiful things with my hands. Until then I will enjoy sitting with her, watching her busy hands as we spend time together.

My nan has busy hands but no matter how busy they are they will always stop to wipe away my tears and give me a hug.

Reading and Comprehension

1. Why does the writer describe her nan's hands as 'busy hands'?

2. Which statement about Nan is invalid?
   (a) She likes to keep busy.
   (b) She has many different skills.
   (c) She is lazy.
   (d) She spends time with her granddaughter.

3. Why does her granddaughter enjoy spending time with Nan?

4. Where does Nan sit and knit?

5. What happens when Nan's hands stop being busy?

6. Which word in the text means skilful?
   (a) embroider (b) plucks (c) dexterous (d) stitches

Spelling and Vocabulary

Rewrite the misspelt words.

7. He mannaged to produce a supreme effert for the last lap of the race.

8. Which golfing achievment of yours do you considor to be the most memrable?

Circle the word that has the nearest meaning to the underlined word.

9. People who continuously lie are <u>detestable</u>.
   (a) likeable (b) attractive (c) denounced (d) hateful

10. This area is a <u>desolate</u> environment.
    (a) saddened (b) deserted (c) populous (d) desert

Circle the correct word in brackets.

11. Do your (draught / draft) copy first on a piece of paper.

12. The work was completed in an efficient (manner / manor).

Grammar and Punctuation

13. Use this **adverbial phrase** in a sentence.
    to complete the work

14. Write in direct speech.
    Many of them said they had finished the work early.

Number and Algebra

1. Write this expansion as one number.
$6 \times 10^0 + 5 \times 10^2 + 6 \times 10^5 + 8 \times 10^3 + 7 \times 10^7 + 2 \times 10^9$ _____

2. Complete.

If $a =$	1	2	3	7	9
$a^2 - 9 =$					

3. Arrange in ascending order.
0.8551, 0.85, 0.855, 0.0085, 0.0058

_____

4. Which numbers are:

(a) three-quarters more than $\frac{5}{8}$? _____

(b) three-sevenths less than $\frac{3}{4}$? _____

5. Mark on this number line: $+4, -3, -5$

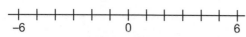

6. $2645 \times 139 =$ _____

7. $17\,488.96 \div 2 =$ _____

8. What is the value of n? _____
$$1\frac{1}{2} + 2\frac{1}{4} = n + 1\frac{3}{8}$$

9. George scored 18 out of 20 in a Science quiz. What was his percentage result? _____

10. The ratio of children to adults is $2:7$. If the population of the town is 1683, how many children are there? _____

11. If the average speed of a car is 5 km/h, what distance would be travelled in t hours? _____

12. How many square metres are there in a rectangle x metres long and 3 metres wide? _____

13. If $m = 9$ and $n = -3$, what is the value of $\frac{m+3}{2n}$? _____

14. Solve $3 + 2a = 10$. _____

Measurement and Space

15. 5% of 1 kg = _____ g

16. The area of a square is $25y^2$ cm². What is the perimeter of the square? _____

17. Calculate the area in m².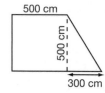

_____

18. Find the volume of a box 22 cm by 9.5 cm by 18 cm. _____

19. In a square-based pyramid there are:

(a) ____ parallel faces (b) ____ vertices

(c) ____ equal faces   (d) one _____

20. Angles a, b and c are supplementary. The ratio of their sizes is $4:2:3$. What is the size of each?

$\angle a =$ _____ $\angle b =$ _____ $\angle c =$ _____

Statistics and Probability

21. What is the probability of drawing a prime number out of the hat?

_____

22. The scores recorded in the stem-and-leaf plot have a range of 28.

Stem	Leaf
4	a7
5	3466
6	022279
7	4

What is the value of a? _____

Advertisement

MACRO TS 1100

The Brand New Australian Motorbike

It's the motorbike you've been waiting for!

- Exhilarating performance on track or road
- Large capacity sports engine
- Sensational styling
- Classic looks
- Cutting edge technology
- Built right here in Australia

Ring 1800 987 6543 for your
nearest dealer to arrange
a test ride today!

Reading and Comprehension

1. The Macro TS 1100 is
   (a) a racing bike.
   (b) a road bike.
   (c) both (a) and (b).
   (d) an off-road bike.

2. Which of the following statements is invalid?
   (a) The bike combines classic looks with latest technology.
   (b) The engine comes from a sporting Japanese bike.
   (c) The motorbike is a very fast machine.
   (d) It has just been released on the Australian market.

3. Which word in the advertisement means 'exciting'?

4. Which two features describe the aesthetics of the bike?

5. Which section of the advertisement implies that the machine is a dual-purpose vehicle?

6. Which phrase indicates that the machine incorporates the latest in features?

Spelling and Vocabulary

Rewrite the misspelt words.

7. Which safty features are emphisised in the motorbike advertisement?

8. This motorbike has an exeptional braking sistem.

Circle the word that has the nearest meaning to the underlined word.

9. What is your appraisal of the new vehicle?
   (a) appreciation   (b) criticism
   (c) opinion   (d) evaluation

10. Trevor had mediocre success as a salesman.
    (a) inferior (b) average (c) superb (d) merit

Circle the correct word in brackets.

11. (Bridal / Bridle) your temper Mary!

12. Many people and (they're / their / there) interests are ignored by advertisers.

Grammar and Punctuation

13. Use this phrase as an adjectival phrase to complete the sentence.

    collecting the machine

    The workers _____

14. Punctuate and capitalise this sentence.

    was the engine for the macro 1100 developed by allen and co in melbourne

Number and Algebra

1. Complete:

$y =$	1	2	3	4	5
$y^2 =$					
$y^3 =$					

2. The letters A and B represent numbers plotted on a number line.
   A is halfway between –7 and –1 and B is halfway between –2 and 6.
   What is $A + B$? _____

3. Make a factor tree for 324. Pair the prime factors
   to find the square root of that number.

4. Write the common fraction $\frac{5}{8}$ as:
   (a) decimal fraction _____
   (b) percentage   _____
   (c) ratio   _____

5. Write the integers that come immediately before and after.
   (a) _____ , –3, _____   (b) _____ , +5, _____
   (c) _____ , –10, _____   (d) _____ , +1, _____

6. $53 + 36 + 72 + 11 = 54 +$ _____ $+ 73 + 10$

7. The number is 20.1283. When rounded off to the nearest hundredth, the number becomes
   0.13, 20.13, 20.12 or 20.1303. Circle the correct answer.

8. A set of golf clubs was sold for $780. There was a discount of $7\frac{1}{2}$%.
   What did the buyer actually pay? _____

9. Which is the greater amount?
   35% of $110 or 27% of $150 _____

10. Simplify $4 : 14 : 24$. _____

11. The algebraic expression $3x + 5 \div y - 2 \times x$ was simplified to $\frac{x + 5}{y}$.
    Use substitution ($x = 3, y = 2$) to decide if this is correct or incorrect.

12. What is the new total when a is doubled and 7 is subtracted from the result? _____

13. $3a - 2ab + ab - 5a$ _____

14. Solve $3p - 6 = 2p + 1$. _____

Measurement and Space

15. What is the difference between 217 kg and 10 t? _____

16. *ABC* is an isosceles triangle. *BC* is half the length of *AC*.
If *AB* is equal to 4.36 m, then what is the perimeter of *ABC*?

_____ m

17. What is the area of the shaded portion?

_____

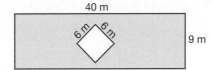

18. One container has a volume of 2.4 litres and the other has a volume of 7.8 litres. How many extra cups, each containing 200 mL, could be filled from the larger container? _____

19. Which one is **not** a pyramid?

_____

A   B   C   D

20. If the measure of angle *ABC* is 80°,
what is the measure of angle *CBE*?

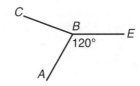

_____

Statistics and Probability

21. Here is a spinner.
If the arrow is spun 20 times, write the most likely number of times a 5 will be spun.

_____

22. Customers at a restaurant are encouraged to rate the quality of their meal using 5 stars.

☆☆☆☆☆

Here are the results of the reviews of 20 customers.

Stars	Customers
0	0
1	0
2	1
3	8
4	5
5	6

What is the mean (average) number of stars?

_____

Stellar Island

The small launch bobbed wildly in the choppy water, like a toy duck in a baby's bath, as the captain steered skilfully towards the rocky, forbidding cove of Stellar Island.

To the two small figures sitting in the bow, the cove appeared to have been carved out of the two sheer, black cliff faces that rose straight up from the sea. The children laughed suddenly as the cold spray splashed over them.

'Patrick and Annabel!' their mother called. 'Come back here!'

The pair reluctantly left the front of the boat and clambered down the small hatch to the cabin below, where their older sister sat quietly on a bench, staring stonily at the water lapping against the porthole.

'What's the matter with Megan?' asked Annabel.

'Nothing', replied her mother. 'Just leave her alone.'

'I'm hungry', announced Patrick. 'Can we have something to eat?'

'We'll be landing in a few minutes. We'll have lunch when we get to the house.' Mrs Kingsley frowned as she looked at her elder daughter, wondering how much longer Megan could keep up this stony silence. It was so unlike her!

The sailor's smiling face suddenly appeared in the hatchway. 'We've arrived, Mrs Kingsley!' he announced cheerfully. 'If you and the children would like to disembark now, we'll bring the luggage up after you.'

The sound of the motor cut out and the boat drifted to a small jetty. It was sheltered from the wind here and the water was reasonably calm.

'Mummy, Patrick's pushing!' Annabel protested as she and Patrick fell over one another trying to be first on deck.

'Stop it, both of you!' Mrs Kingsley snapped.

Megan followed more slowly, helping her mother to carry their hand luggage.

This is it, she thought as she climbed out of the cabin. My prison for the next year.

But in the space of a minute her gloom lifted. There was her father, smiling and waving from the jetty. How she'd missed him over the past few weeks! He looked so fit and happy too. Well, if life on the island had done so much for him in such a short space of time, maybe—just maybe— it wasn't going to be so bad after all.

There was a lot of commotion for a while as everyone hugged and kissed and talked, all at once.

'Okay, okay!' Mr Kingsley laughed. 'Gimme a break!' He led them, still chattering and falling over one another, along a path which meandered away from the cove.

It was a steep climb and by the time they reached the top everyone was out of breath. Dropping their assorted bags and luggage, the children collapsed on to a grassy patch.

'Jerry and the boys will bring everything up, Bev', said Mr Kingsley. 'It won't take them too long.' He pointed to a low bank of thick cloud on the horizon. 'They'll want to get away before the storm comes.'

'What's the house like?' asked Megan.

'I think you'll be surprised.' He swung Annabel onto his shoulders. 'Come on, all you lazybones! The sooner you get there, the sooner you'll find out!'

There was another commotion as they scrambled for their things.

'I'm glad we're all together again', said Patrick as he ran ahead. 'This is going to be great!'

Mrs Kingsley and Megan lagged behind. 'Darling, you know Daddy and I wouldn't drag you off somewhere where we thought you'd be unhappy.'

'I know, Mum. It's just a bit strange, that's all.' Megan managed a small grin. 'Isn't it great to see Dad looking so good!'

They followed the others, so immersed in their own thoughts that neither of them noticed a slight figure emerge from behind a rock.

The girl watched impassively as the new lighthouse keeper and his family made their way up to the old house.

From *The Incredible Experience of Megan Kingsley* by Pamela O'Connor

Reading and Comprehension

1. The launch was heading
    (a) across the bay to a secluded beach.
    (b) towards a small jetty.
    (c) into a rocky cove.
    (d) both (b) and (c)

2. Mrs Kingsley and her children were travelling
    (a) to an isolated area for a vacation.
    (b) to visit friends they had not seen recently.
    (c) to begin a new life as a lighthouse keeper's family.
    (d) to visit the lighthouse and the surrounding area.

3. Megan was very quiet because
    (a) she was very tired after the long trip.
    (b) she was not looking forward to the change.
    (c) she was quite hungry.
    (d) the other children were bothering her.

4. How does the author suggest a mystery that will be solved?

_____

_____

_____

5. Why did Megan's gloomy mood leave her when she climbed out of the cabin?

_____

_____

6. Why would the children have been immersed in their own thoughts as they walked up to the lighthouse?

_____

_____

_____

Spelling and Vocabulary

Rewrite the misspelt words.

7. The jetty was shelterd from the wind and reasonabley calm.

_____

8. The children colappsed on the grassey patch.

_____

Circle the word that has the nearest meaning to the underlined word.

9. They <u>reluctantly</u> left the front of the boat.
    (a) carefully
    (b) restlessly
    (c) probably
    (d) unwillingly

10. The girl was watching <u>impassively</u> as the people made their way up to the house.
    (a) seriously
    (b) impatiently
    (c) serenely
    (d) quietly

Circle the correct word in brackets.

11. There was a (sleight / slight) figure emerging from behind the rock.

12. The cove had been carved out of two (shear / sheer) black cliff faces.

Grammar and Punctuation

13. Use *to mend the nets* as an adjectival clause to complete this sentence.

    The child _____

_____

_____.

14. Write in indirect speech.

    'We'll go up to the old house first', she replied.

_____

_____

_____

_____

© 1999 Harval Pty Ltd and Pascal Press
Reprinted 2000, 2001, 2002, 2003, 2004, 2006, 2007, 2008, 2009, 2010, 2012

Updated in 2013 for the Australian Curriculum

Reprinted 2014, 2017, 2018, 2019, 2021, 2022, 2023

Updated in 2024 for the NSW Curriculum and Australian Curriculum Version 9.0 changes

ISBN 978 1 86441 335 9

Pascal Press
PO Box 250
Glebe NSW 2037
(02) 9198 1748
www.pascalpress.com.au

Publisher: Vivienne Joannou
Australian Curriculum updates edited by Rosemary Peers
Answers checked by Peter Little, Dale Little and Melinda Amaral
Typeset by Precision Typesetting (Barbara Nilsson), and lj Design (Julianne Billington) and
    Grizzly Graphics (Leanne Richters)
Cover by DiZign Pty Ltd
Additional writing by Dale Little
Printed by Vivar Printing/Green Giant Press

Acknowledgements
The following sources for material are kindly acknowledged:
'Andy's Gone With Cattle' by Henry Lawson
From the 'Spectrum' series, HBJ:
Golden Wombats by Jill Morris
Ho, Ho, Ho! by Jan Weeks
Additional Fables by Rolf Grunseit
Charlie's Fish by RL Muddyman
Homeland Australia by Michael Dugan
Night of the Muttonbirds by Mary Small
Legends of our Land by Oodgeroo Noonuccal
TV News by Elizabeth Halley
Strange Mysteries by Rachael Collinson
Sport in the Making by Shane Power
Shaping the News by John Fitzgerald
Framing Ned Kelly by Louise Martin-Chew
That Smell is my Brother! by Bill Condon
What a Waste! by Stephen Jones
Puppets by Carole Hooper
The Incredible Experience of Megan Kingsley by Pamela O'Connor